MW00422681

Campus Free Speech

Campus
Free
Speech

A Pocket Guide

CASS R. SUNSTEIN

Harvard University Press
Cambridge, Massachusetts · London, England · 2024

Publication of this book has been supported through the
generous provisions of the S. M. Bessie Fund.

LIBRARY OF CONGRESS CATALOGING-IN-PUBLICATION DATA

Names: Sunstein, Cass R., author.
Title: Campus free speech : a pocket guide / Cass R. Sunstein.
Description: Cambridge, Massachusetts : Harvard University Press, 2024. |
Includes bibliographical references and index. |
Identifiers: LCCN 2024019059 (print) | LCCN 2024019060 (ebook) | ISBN
9780674298781 (cloth) | ISBN 9780674298804 (epub) |
ISBN 9780674298798 (pdf)
Subjects: LCSH: Freedom of speech—United States. | Academic
Freedom—United States. | Universities and colleges—Law and
Legislation—United States.
Classification: LCC KF4772 .S87 2024 (print) | LCC KF4772 (ebook) |
DDC 342.7308/53—dc23/eng/20240523
LC record available at https://lccn.loc.gov/2024019059
LC ebook record available at https://lccn.loc.gov/2024019060

To Geoffrey Stone and Edward Glaeser,
admired friends and apostles of freedom

Contents

Preface

I have spent most of my life at a university. For twenty-seven years, I was lucky enough to teach at the University of Chicago, a home for diverse views among students and faculty alike. Left, right, and center—all were welcome there. While I was at Chicago, giants walked the earth. The Monsters of the Midway believed, above all, in uninhibited debate.

The Department of Economics featured Gary Becker and George Stigler, Nobel Prize winners passionately devoted to freedom of expression. Becker was short and Stigler was tall. Becker was often puzzled; Stigler was never puzzled. They were close colleagues and vigorous debaters.

Becker and Stigler were unmistakably right of center, but they focused on academic research, not politics. Becker was a hero of mine, not only because he was brilliant and creative, but also because he was endlessly curious. He was both fierce and respectful. Despite his high standards and toughness, he was generous and kind. Confronted with a new idea, he would ask, with a quizzical expression: "How would we test that?" That question has stuck in my mind for decades.

Becker was skeptical of behavioral economics, one of my fields, but he really wanted to understand it, and to see how to make the best of it. Stigler was gleeful and acerbic, and he could be cutting. When I gave a paper on paternalism, an early work at the intersection of behavioral economics and law, at the famous and terrifying Becker-Stigler workshop, Stigler prefaced a question to me by saying, "What you're saying reminds me of an argument by John Stuart Mill. What you're saying is almost as stupid as what he said." Stigler was funny and sharp. He made everyone around him better.

The University of Chicago Law School was, and is, a treasure. During my years there, the pantheon featured Richard Posner, Frank Easterbrook, Antonin Scalia, Elena Kagan, Diane Wood, Bernard Meltzer, Richard Epstein, Geoffrey Stone, Thomas Miles, Hans Zeisel, Larry Lessig, David Strauss, Martha Nussbaum, Eric Posner, and many others. Most of those names won't mean anything to you, and some of them are no longer among us, but they are all alive to me. (It feels as if they are in the room with me as I write.) In that crowd, freedom of speech was a given. It was not questioned. You could make any argument you liked, and everything depended on whether you could support what you had to say. Nothing, left or right, was politically incorrect.

Chicago was a bit like the Constitutional Convention as described by James Madison: "Meantime the minds of the members were changing, and much was to be gained by a yielding and accommodating spirit. . . . [N]o man felt himself obliged to retain his opinions any longer than he was satisfied of their propriety and truth, and was open to the force of argument." If Chicago's guiding spirit was not always "yielding and accommodating," it was at least one of openness and curiosity. It is no accident that two appendices to this book come from the University of Chicago.

Since 2008, I have taught at Harvard, with two stints in the federal government. Harvard Law School, my principal home, has its own giants: Stephen Breyer, Louis Kaplow, Randy Kennedy, John Goldberg, Steven Shavell, Oren Bar-Gill, John Manning, Mary Ann Glendon, Jack Goldsmith, Steve Sachs, Martha Minow, Charles Fried, Lawrence Tribe, Daphna Renan, and many others. These are not people who agree with one another! I am also lucky enough to be affiliated with the Department of Economics, with such superstars as Edward Glaeser, David Laibson, Benjamin Enke, Matthew Rabin, Claudia Goldin, Andrei Shleifer, and Amartya Sen. I am in awe of every one of them. At Harvard's Law School and its Department of Economics, freedom of speech is also a given. It is not questioned. Everything depends on the force of the argument.

But at some American colleges and universities (I will refer to both as "universities" for short), freedom of speech is not at all a given. It is questioned. Censorship is in place. Some views are out of bounds. Maybe you can't be on the left; maybe you can't be on the right; maybe you can't be in between. People are being punished because of what they say. Some of the restrictions come from universities themselves, and some from public officials outside the universities.

Let me put some cards on the table: I don't like that at all. During World War II, when freedom was under assault all over the world, Justice Robert Jackson produced the greatest sentence ever written by a member of the United States Supreme Court: "Compulsory unification of opinion achieves only the unanimity of the graveyard."[1] There are different kinds of graveyards. All of them are quiet.

Freedom of speech is essential to self-government and to personal autonomy. It is necessary for learning. It performs a checking function; it helps to prevent and correct error. It shows respect for people. It helps all of us to find our own way. It combats mindless conformity. The United States aspires to be a deliberative democracy, one that combines accountability with reason-giving, and freedom of speech makes deliberative democracy possible. Freedom of speech is important even in systems that are not democratic. It produces experiments. It shows that long-held beliefs may be false. (The earth really does go around the sun.) It puts things up for grabs. It inculcates humility, and also confidence.

Still, educational institutions are distinctive, even unique. The educational mission will require an assortment of restrictions on speech. You can't run a college or a university without imposing such restrictions. What restrictions? It's complicated. You'll see.

Introduction

Imagine that students on a university campus are protesting "the dismal state of civil rights in the United States." They are angry and they are loud. They chant. They are also disruptive. They march through the campus with signs saying such things as "Racist from the Start," "The University Is Complicit," "Slavery Was Never Abolished," and "Justice Here, Justice Now!" Some of the signs are more (shall we say) provocative than that. They contain four-letter words.

Many students, faculty, and alumni are offended. They want the university to "shut this nonsense down." Should it do that? Can it?

Here is the text of the First Amendment to the United States Constitution:

> Congress shall make no law respecting an establishment of religion, or prohibiting the free exercise thereof; or abridging the freedom of speech, or of the press; or the right of the people peaceably to assemble, and to petition the Government for a redress of grievances.[1]

Here is a sentence from the Fourteenth Amendment to the United States Constitution:

> No State shall make or enforce any law which shall abridge the privileges or immunities of citizens of the United States; nor shall any State deprive any person of life, liberty, or property, without due process of law; nor deny to any person within its jurisdiction the equal protection of the laws.[2]

As you can immediately see, the First Amendment applies only to "Congress." It does not apply to colleges and universities. But the Supreme Court has ruled that the Fourteenth Amendment "incorporates" the First Amendment, which means that states, and not just Congress, are bound by it.[3] That means in turn that public colleges and universities, whether state or federal, are bound by it, too. Let us focus on seven words from the First Amendment: "no law . . . abridging the freedom of speech." They are my topic here.

You might be tempted to think that those seven words call for a kind of free speech absolutism. Isn't the phrase "no law abridging" quite clear? But things are not nearly so simple. Is a law forbidding bribery or perjury, or libel or blasphemy, a "law abridging"? Maybe not. And what is "the freedom of speech," anyway? Does it include commercial advertising, threats, obscenity, or criminal solicitation? Maybe not. The words are ambiguous. To interpret them, we need a theory of interpretation.

In constitutional law, people vigorously disagree about what counts as the right theory. Should we be bound by the "original public meaning" of the document, that is, the meaning of the words as they were understood when ratified? Many people, including some members of the Supreme Court, think so. Or should we understand "the freedom of speech" as a general principle whose specific meaning evolves over time? Many people, including some members of the Supreme Court, think so. Should we understand "the freedom of speech" in part by reference to principles of equality? Many people, including some members of the Supreme Court, think so, too. These are disputed questions, and I am not going to answer them here.[4] Instead I am going to take existing free speech law, as laid down by the Supreme Court, as given. In doing so, I am not suffering; on these issues, I like existing law a lot.[5]

I have noted that public colleges and universities are part of government, usually state government, which means that they are bound by the First Amendment. They are required to follow it. If they suppress speech, they might be imposing a "law abridging the freedom of speech." The University of Minnesota, the University of Massachusetts, and the University of Michigan, among countless others, must follow the Constitution. The same is true of the legislatures and executive officials, both federal and state, who might try to regulate what universities do.

By contrast, private colleges and universities are not bound by the Constitution. Many people are surprised to hear this; some people are shocked. But schools such as Harvard University, Stanford University, Columbia University, Oberlin College, Boston College, and Trinity College can regulate speech as they like, at least in the sense that the First Amendment does not apply to them.

As far as the Constitution is concerned, they can censor people.[6] If they wish, they can embrace a right-of-center ideology and prohibit students and faculty from saying anything that is inconsistent with it. They might declare a "war on woke." They might adopt a firm rule: faculty and students are forbidden to say anything unpatriotic. Or they might embrace the left, and forbid students and faculty from questioning left-wing ideology. They might proclaim that negative remarks about people based on their religion, gender, race, age, or sexual orientation are "microaggressions," and will not be tolerated on campus.

In my view, no university should do these kinds of things. Universities are institutions of higher learning, and if they do not allow a lot of free speech, there will not be enough learning. There should be no wars on "woke" and no wars on right-of-center thought. Diverse views and exchanges of opinion are essential to the educational enterprise. There was a time when almost everyone thought, with great confidence, that the sun went around the earth. There was a time when people thought that if you want to improve your vision, you should eat a lot of carrots. There was a time when people thought that a woman's place was in the home. There was a time when people thought, with great confidence, that slavery was acceptable. Here's how Justice Oliver Wendell Holmes put it:

> Persecution for the expression of opinions seems to me perfectly logical. If you have no doubt of your premises or your power, and want a certain result with all your heart, you naturally express your wishes in law, and sweep away

all opposition. To allow opposition by speech seems to indicate that you think the speech impotent, as when a man says that he has squared the circle, or that you do not care wholeheartedly for the result, or that you doubt either your power or your premises. But when men have realized that time has upset many fighting faiths, they may come to believe even more than they believe the very foundations of their own conduct that the ultimate good desired is better reached by free trade in ideas—that the best test of truth is the power of the thought to get itself accepted in the competition of the market, and that truth is the only ground upon which their wishes safely can be carried out. That, at any rate, is the theory of our Constitution. It is an experiment, as all life is an experiment.[7]

Time has indeed upset many fighting faiths. With Holmes's views in mind, many private colleges and universities might decide that they should *voluntarily* comply with the First Amendment; they might believe that that is the right thing to do.[8] This is, I think, an honorable idea, and it is more right than wrong, though I will raise some questions about it. For the moment, let us focus on these questions: Insofar as public or private universities are regulating speech, what may they do, if they are to follow the First Amendment? What are they forbidden to do?

A word on scope: As you can see, my focus is on the United States Constitution and hence on American law. I am daring to hope, however, that the discussion will be of international interest as well.

Austria and Australia, South Korea and South Africa, Germany and Ghana, India and Indonesia—every country with higher education faces its own questions about freedom of speech on campus.

Appendix A offers a brief framework that universities might consider as a starting point for formulating their own approach to free speech on campus. The principles sketched here will not suit everyone. But I am hopeful that they will suit many, and that even when some of them are rejected, others might be found attractive, in whole or in part. In any case, engaging with ideas and traditions that one does not accept is often an excellent idea. Indeed, it is a major reason for being at a university in the first place.

Some General Points

Before we get to specifics, it is essential to keep a few general points in mind.

Norms and Sanctions

If a university is seeking to restrict speech, it might act in many ways. Students might be suspended; their grades might be lowered; they might not receive course credit; they might be expelled. Teachers might be suspended; their salaries might be frozen or lowered; they might be fined; their teaching and administrative duties might be altered or curtailed; they might be discharged. In all of these cases, we are speaking of sanctions, understood as formal punishments. They are the topic of this book.

Norms are very different.[1] In ordinary life, people follow many norms that are not enforced by formal sanctions. If you are unkind, you might be violating a norm, but you will not be punished in any official way. So, too, a university might insist that it seeks to maintain a certain kind of culture, in which people follow norms of considerateness, civility, and respect.[2] If faculty or students violate those norms, someone might talk to them and give them some kind of reminder (perhaps informal, perhaps firm). If a student uses vulgar words in class, a teacher might suggest that the student should stop doing that, without imposing any kind of punishment. When I was a young faculty member at the University of Chicago Law School and angry at an older colleague, a contemporary of mine, wise beyond his years, said: "Cass, a faculty is like a family. Sure, you can be mad, but try to get over it, and don't act out." Not long ago, a student of mine used a profanity (the word began with f) in a class of about three hundred students; I offered a mild rebuke, suggesting that the student had made an unusual word choice. Norms often do the work of law. Universities need a lot of them.

Norms are essential to social life, including academic life. On campus, good norms are required for productive exchanges. Bad norms can be an obstacle to such exchanges. We could imagine a wide variety of norms. A university might encourage sharp, even unpleasant debates and insist that what matters is the pursuit of truth, not civility. It might welcome aggression, even if some people's feelings get hurt. (That is what I saw at the University of Chicago Law School.) A university might insist on seeking truth, but also put a premium on generosity and kindness. (I have seen that at Yale Law School.) But so long as no one is being sanctioned, and so long as people remain able to say what they like, norms do not raise free speech questions under the Constitution. When speech is hurtful or harmful, an insistence on norms is often the right response.

It is true, of course, that some norms might work to suppress speech by discouraging people from saying what they think. Norms of conformity can have a horrific effect on personal freedom.[3] It is both important and challenging to produce norms that strike the right balance. But my topic here is the Constitution, and norms that are not enforced by law cannot offend it.

Clear and Present Danger

What if speech is likely to produce violence? What if it is likely to produce unlawful action, such as a takeover of a university building? Under the First Amendment, public institutions may punish speech that is "directed to inciting or producing imminent lawless action and is likely to incite or produce such action."[4] That formulation, adopted in the defining case of *Brandenburg v. Ohio,* is the modern incarnation of the clear-and-present-danger test.[5] Public universities may punish speech that runs afoul of the test.

It is important to see that the test has four elements:

1. *Likelihood* that the action will occur
2. *Intention* of the speaker to incite that action ("directed to inciting")
3. *Imminence* of the action
4. *Lawlessness* of the action

Speech that condones or counsels violence is not regulable if (for example) such violence is not "likely" to occur.[6] Suppose that someone cries out, "Let's take over a building!" Or suppose that someone says, "Let's overthrow the government!" Such comments may not be punished if nothing is "likely" to happen as a result of those words. What does "likely" mean? Under common understandings, it means more probable than not—at least 50.1 percent likely to occur. If the likelihood of violence is 40 percent, regulation is not permissible. And what if the speaker does not *intend* to incite violence, though violence is exactly what he is inciting? Under current law, the speaker cannot be regulated.

It is reasonable to ask whether the *Brandenburg* framework might be softened or refined in the university setting, consistent with the First Amendment. In other words, it might be suggested that universities should have more freedom to regulate speech than the *Brandenburg* framework allows. What if the likelihood of violence is 48 percent? That is a fair question. For the moment, notice a simple point: if speech *is* regulable under the *Brandenburg* framework, it is certainly regulable on campus.

Unprotected Speech

Brandenburg is sufficient to show that certain categories of speech are not protected by the First Amendment at all. Some people claim to be free speech absolutists, but as we have seen, absolutism with respect to free speech is hard to defend, whatever your theory of interpretation. Consider this statement: "Your money or your life!" Or how about this one: "Let's conspire to fix prices." Or this one: "Unless you sleep with me, you will get a terrible grade in this course." Or this one, from a professor of English literature: "The problem with having Asian students in literature courses is—well, don't get me started!"

False commercial advertising can be forbidden, and the same is true of obscenity, bribery, defamation and libel (subject to prevailing constitutional standards), "true threats," sexual harassment (properly defined), criminal solicitation, perjury, child pornography, and fraud.[7] There is no constitutional right to plagiarize.[8] There is no constitutional right to violate copyright laws (though we can imagine particular cases in which plausible First Amendment objections are raised).[9] There is no constitutional right to use ChatGPT or other large language models (LLMs) to write papers or exam answers.[10]

Why is some speech unprotected? There is no uniform theory, but the basic idea is simple: some speech has "low value," in the sense that it is disconnected from the central values of the First Amendment, which include self-government and personal autonomy. If one person threatens to hurt another, or sexually harasses another, those central values are not at stake. At the same time, the government typically has a solid or strong justification for regulating the relevant speech. In the cases of threats and sexual harassment, or bribery, defamation, perjury, child pornography, and fraud, the strength of the justification is self-evident.

It is worth repeating: universities are allowed to punish unprotected speech.[11] That is an exceedingly important conclusion. It suggests that many cases will be easy cases. We will see a bunch of them.

Three Kinds of Restrictions

For those concerned about free speech on campus, it is important to distinguish among three kinds of restrictions on what people may say: viewpoint-based, content-based, and content-neutral.[12] A viewpoint-based restriction is one that punishes people because of the point of view that they express. For example, such a restriction might say that while students may praise the president of the university, they may not criticize the president of the university. Or it might say that students may not make disrespectful statements about their teachers, with an understanding that respectful statements are permitted (and most welcome).

A content-based restriction is one that targets or punishes people because of the content of their speech. All viewpoint-based restrictions are content-based, but some content-based restrictions are viewpoint-neutral. For example, a university might say that students cannot discuss an ongoing war, whatever they propose to say about it. Or a university might say that students cannot discuss religion over dinner.

A content-neutral restriction applies regardless of what is being said. A "time, place, and manner" restriction would count as content-neutral. For example, such a restriction might say that between the hours of midnight and six AM, no loud talking of any kind will be allowed in dormitories. A content-neutral restriction applies to all points of view, and to know whether it is violated, we do not need to know anything about the content of the relevant speech.

In general, viewpoint-based restrictions face a strong presumption of invalidity.[13] They are usually struck down. New York cannot ban speech that says nasty things about the governor while allowing speech that says nice things about the governor. Alabama cannot ban speech that supports critical race theory while allowing speech that condemns critical race theory. Texas cannot enact legislation that embodies a "war on woke," at least not if it is viewpoint-based (and it sounds pretty viewpoint-based). To be sure, we might be able to imagine cases in which a viewpoint-based restriction is acceptable. Someone might be prevented from saying "kill that man" when there is an imminent threat of violence, even if they are not prevented from saying "do not kill that man." Someone might be forbidden from saying "let's fix prices," even if they are not forbidden from saying "let's not fix prices."[14] In the context of a serious, imminent threat to public safety or national security, certain kinds of speech might be banned because of their viewpoint. As we will see, the educational setting raises distinctive questions. But in general, viewpoint-based restrictions are impermissible.

Content-based restrictions also face a heavy burden of justification, even if they are viewpoint-neutral, and they are usually struck down.[15] A state cannot forbid people from discussing civil rights or an ongoing war effort. But the heavy burden of justification can sometimes be met in the educational setting, not least because education necessarily involves the establishment of content (and so content-based judgments). Universities can tell history professors that they have to teach history, not geometry, in their history courses. Universities can tell students that in courses on World War II, their papers and exams have to focus on World War II, not on animal rights.

Content-neutral restrictions, such as time, place, and manner restrictions, are subject to a balancing test.[16] The balancing test is described in different ways, but in practice, it depends largely on four factors:

1. The strength of the interest in preventing the speech (is the goal to prevent a genuinely serious problem or to eliminate a minor inconvenience?)
2. The extent of the adverse effect of the regulation on people's ability to communicate (is the adverse effect small or large?)
3. The presence of alternative ways, or channels, by which people can get their message across
4. The possibility that officials can achieve their legitimate goals through means that are less restrictive of speech (is the restriction "narrowly tailored"?)

Consider two polar examples.

1. A content-neutral prohibition on all public demonstrations on campus except between the hours of 3:00 AM and 3:15 AM would fail the balancing test. Such a prohibition cuts very broadly; it comes close to banning public demonstrations. For that reason, it would have a serious harmful effect on people's ability to communicate. It is far from clear why a university

would find it necessary or important to do that. The university's interest in imposing such a broad restriction seems weak.

2. A content-neutral prohibition on shouting in dormitories between the hours of midnight and six AM would be upheld. Such a prohibition would serve an important interest: ensuring that students get to sleep. And if people cannot shout in dormitories during those hours, surely they can find other ways to make themselves heard.

Consideration of the four factors might seem unacceptably unruly, but in practice it is quite orderly. We can easily find cases like the first, in which a content-neutral restriction is preventing a lot of speech for no sufficient reason. We can easily find cases like the second, in which a content-neutral restriction is evidently justified. We can easily find hard cases, too, and we will be able to know why they are hard: the restriction is not trivial, and it is not clear if the university's interest is sufficient to justify it. We will see some hard cases below.

Due Process and Fair Notice

People are entitled to due process and fair notice, which means that they should not be subject to unfair surprise. That principle protects faculty, students, and administrators alike. Even if speech is regulable, universities would be well advised to ensure that people are genuinely on notice about what particular kinds of speech might subject them to controls or sanctions.[17] Universities should, in short, describe what they intend to prohibit with a high degree of clarity, so as to let people know what is off-limits.

The first reason for such clarity is to ensure that people know what they can and cannot say and do. The second reason is to avoid arbitrariness on the part of those who are charged with enforcing the restriction. The word "arbitrariness" points to two distinct problems of its own. The first is invidiousness; the second is randomness. If the authorities are allowed to adopt an open-ended restriction, they might go after people whom they dislike (perhaps because of the opinions those people express, perhaps because of the color of their skin). Or they might exercise their discretion in random or unpredictable ways. Speakers might find themselves in a lottery in which they end up as losers.

A standard that forbids "discourtesy," "inappropriate speech," "incivility," "misconduct," or "unreasonable behavior" might well be unduly open-ended.[18] Such broad terms might not tell people what they need to avoid. I shall have something to say about this problem in a few places, but it can arise in essentially all cases.

There is a related point. The First Amendment not only forbids unacceptable vagueness; it also forbids "overbreadth." A regulation that bans "incitement to criminal activity" might not be vague; perhaps the terms are well defined. But it is overbroad, in the sense that it forbids some speech that the First Amendment protects. (Recall that under the *Brandenburg* framework, people cannot be punished for calling for illegal action, if listeners are highly unlikely to pay attention to their call.) Under some circumstances, a restriction that is overly broad, in the sense that it threatens to punish protected speech, might be struck down for that very reason.

It is easy to confuse vagueness and overbreadth, but they are distinct concepts. To see why, suppose that a law makes it a crime to "engage in speech that is unprotected by the First Amendment." Such a law cannot possibly be overbroad; it protects all speech that the First Amendment protects. But in all probability, it is unconstitutionally vague! The reason is that First Amendment law is pretty messy, and it would not provide people with fair notice about what they can and cannot say.

The Educational Mission

Universities have a distinctive mission. Here things get especially interesting, and also really complicated.

COMMON GROUND

Let us begin with what should be common ground: universities should be, and are, permitted to regulate speech *if the regulation is genuinely essential to their educational mission.*[19] For example, a university is permitted to insist that law professors seeking tenure in their field focus on law, not on French literature. So too, a university is permitted to tell students that they must wait their turn to speak in class. It is in some sense true that across a broad territory, students and faculty ought to be permitted to say what they like. In that sense, they are free from the constraining arm of public officials. At the same time, universities must be able to carry out their educational mission, which means that they should have some authority over speech that most government institutions lack. The point is connected with the idea of academic freedom (on which more below).

The phrase "genuinely essential to their educational mission" is regrettably vague, might be criticized as too narrow or too broad, requires specification, and leaves a great deal open for discussion and debate.[20] Nonetheless, it points in the right direction. Because of their distinctive missions, some public institutions are allowed to regulate the speech of their employees. The Department of State is allowed to forbid high-level employees from going on television to offer their private opinions on immigration questions, and the Department of Defense is allowed to forbid speech by its employees that castigates high-level political officials, such as the secretary of defense and the president. The Hatch Act broadly restricts political activities by federal officials, and it is consistent with the First Amendment. (Look it up, if you like.)

Something similar holds for educational institutions, including universities. It follows that the presumption against content discrimination must be approached with some caution in the educational setting, and the same is even true for the presumption against viewpoint discrimination.[21] If that seems alarming, consider a few examples. If a student answers a history test about the Peloponnesian War with an essay on the superiority of Michael Jordan to LeBron James, or of Christians to Muslims, the professor may flunk that student. Even if an English professor would like to discuss climate change rather than Shakespeare in a course on Shakespeare, a university is entitled to insist that she stick to the subject of her course. A more controversial case: if a math professor believes that men are better than women at math and that women cannot handle the subject, there is a good argument that he can be directed not to say that in class, on the grounds that if he does so, he will not be able to do his job. (There is a difference between what professors may say in class and what they may say out of class.)

No First Amendment problem arises if a teacher gives a low grade, or a flunking grade, to a student who tries to defend the proposition that the earth is flat or that the sun goes around the earth, even if the professor is engaging in content discrimination or viewpoint discrimination. The educational enterprise permits institutions to impose restrictions that would not be acceptable if imposed by, for example, the national government. The national government cannot punish you for arguing that men are better than women in math, or that the earth is flat.

Least controversially, subject-matter restrictions are often permissible. In some cases, viewpoint discrimination may raise hard questions. What if a student writes a term paper defending Hitler? Can the fact that the paper defends Hitler count against a good grade? What if an assistant professor writes a celebratory book about rape? Can such a book count against tenure? The simplest thing to say is that work can be evaluated on its merits, and a defense of Hitler or of rape is unlikely to be any good. But viewpoint-neutral evaluation of work on such topics might not be so easy.

PICKERING

However we deal with the hardest questions, the central proposition—that educational institutions can act to regulate speech if the act is essential to protect their mission—is a reasonable inference from *Pickering v. Board of Education.*[22] *Pickering* is the leading case on the First Amendment rights of public employees. The case happened to involve a teacher, and it has a host of implications for free speech on campus. Let's spend some time with it.

Marvin Pickering, a science teacher in Lockport, Illinois, was discharged for writing a letter to a newspaper in which he was sharply critical of decisions of the local board of education and the district superintendent of schools, objecting to how they had decided to raise new revenue. According to the board, the letter contained numerous falsehoods and unjustifiably impugned the "motives, honesty, integrity, truthfulness, responsibility and competence" of both the board and the school administration. For that reason, they urged, it was permissible to discharge him.

The Supreme Court ruled that Pickering's discharge violated the First Amendment. The Court began by noting that public employees, including teachers, retain constitutional rights, and they do not waive those rights by accepting employment. Crucially, Pickering's letter involved not private or internal matters, but issues of legitimate public concern. Also crucially, the letter was not directed at any particular person with whom Pickering "would normally be in contact in the course of his daily work as a teacher. Thus, no question of maintaining either discipline by immediate superiors or harmony among coworkers is presented here."[23]

To be sure, the letter contained falsehoods, but they could not be shown to have been harmful. The statements made by Pickering were "neither shown nor can be presumed to have in any way either impeded the teacher's proper performance of his daily duties in the classroom or to have interfered with the regular operation of the schools generally."[24] In the Court's view, "the interest of the school administration in limiting teachers' opportunities to contribute to public debate is not significantly greater than its interest in limiting a similar contribution by any member of the general public."[25] Note the implication of the Court's analysis: if Pickering's letter *had* impeded his proper performance, or interfered with the regular operation of the school, the outcome might be different. That point suggests that universities, as universities, might be able to punish or deter speech if such steps are necessary to ensure that teachers can do their jobs. That idea requires elaboration, but for the moment, let's simply plant a flag.

The approach in *Pickering* was refined in *Connick v. Myers,* involving not teachers but an assistant district attorney.[26] The case arose when prosecutor Sheila Myers was informed that she would be transferred to a different section of the criminal court. Resisting the transfer, she produced a questionnaire that she distributed to other assistant district attorneys in the office, asking about office morale, the need for a grievance committee, the level of confidence in supervisors, and transfer policy. At that point, she was discharged. The Court upheld the discharge, clarifying that as an employer, the government has broad authority to discharge employees for speaking on matters of private rather than public concern, at least where the relevant speech would disrupt close working relationships or otherwise make it difficult for the relevant workplace to continue to operate efficiently.

With respect to the rights of teachers, a general implication of *Pickering* and *Connick* is that it matters whether university authorities are acting in their distinctive capacity as *employers,* trying to ensure that the university functions well, or instead in their capacity as *government officials,* trying to restrict speech that people find objectionable or offensive. The distinction is also relevant to the rights of students. This is not the simplest line to draw, but as we shall see, it tends to become clear in the context of particular cases.

A CHALLENGE

I am operating here within the boundaries of First Amendment law, but today's boundaries can of course become tomorrow's open field. Some people might think that the educational mission has much larger implications than I am going to allow. Consider, for example, a brilliant analysis by Robert Post, former dean of Yale Law School. It is worthwhile lingering over Post's analysis, not only because it is powerful and intriguing, but also because it points toward a possible path for the future—though not the best one, in my view. In short, Post would emphasize academic freedom and the educational mission of the university in a way that would, I fear, allow too much in the way of regulation of speech on campus.

Post urges that First Amendment principles are fundamentally designed for "public discourse" and for "the formation of public opinion."[27] In his account, "we are not the free authors of our own government if we are compelled to participate in the formation of public opinion in a manner that is contrary to our own will."[28] Fair enough, and well put. To this extent, Post does not mean to question the basic principles that I shall be invoking here. But in his account, those principles were not designed for, and do not fit, the university setting at all. Let us listen to him:

> The purpose of classic First Amendment principles is to protect the process of self-government. But speech within universities does not serve this purpose. It serves the purpose of education, which requires an entirely different framework of speech regulation and protection. Speech within campus is ordinarily protected according to principles of academic freedom, as distinct from freedom of speech.[29]

To support these conclusions, Post notes that on campus, content discrimination is pervasive: "If I am supposed to be teaching constitutional law, I can't spend my classroom time talking about auto mechanics."[30] Academic freedom, which Post means to highlight, is not the same as the classic First Amendment tradition: "Freedom of teaching is not about self-government; it is about education."[31] Post thinks that insofar as they are being applied to campus settings, First Amendment principles are being "overexten[ded]."[32]

In my view, Post is on firm ground insofar as he is suggesting that the educational mission is highly relevant to an assessment of whether restrictions on speech are permissible—just as the missions of the Department of Defense, the Central Intelligence Agency, and the Corporation for Public Broadcasting are relevant to an assessment of whether restrictions on speech by those institutions are permissible. We could indeed "overextend" First Amendment principles if (for example) we said that universities cannot insist that students and professors spend class time on the topic of the class. As I have suggested, the general requirement of content neutrality must be softened in the university setting, which also places some pressure on the general requirement of viewpoint neutrality.

But I do not agree with Post's suggestion that we should jettison "classic First Amendment principles" in favor of "principles of academic freedom." He does not spell out the implications of that suggestion, but if we jettison First Amendment principles, some of the core safeguards, including the presumptive ban on viewpoint discrimination, would be in jeopardy. Free speech would be at risk in a place where it needs to flourish. As we have seen, the ban on viewpoint discrimination cannot always be firm in the university setting. But still, the ban on viewpoint discrimination is *often* firm on campus—and essential. The classic principles should, in my view, not only be retained; they should be celebrated.

In any case, it is not entirely clear that the Constitution broadly protects academic freedom as such. That is a complicated matter. The idea of academic freedom often refers to a kind of norm or background principle: *Within a broad range, universities should be able to do as they like. Their freedom, and their independence, have a great deal of social value.* We should be prepared to agree that certain government intrusions on academic institutions, and on the freedom of those who are part of them, are unconstitutional.[33] No one should doubt that if and when government interferes with the judgments of academic institutions ("No university shall teach that evolution is true"), there is likely to be a serious First Amendment issue, if and when such interference impairs freedom of speech. Interference of that kind is especially objectionable if it is viewpoint-based.

To that extent, some forms of academic freedom are incorporated within classic First Amendment principles. Those classic principles remain relevant to the assessment of when universities themselves may interfere with freedom of speech. The *Report of the Committee on Freedom of Expression* from the University of Chicago, given in Appendix B, seems founded on that view, and it seems to me to be fundamentally right. (The suggested framework given in Appendix A seems to me entirely right, but then again I am biased in its favor.)

Equally important, the classic First Amendment principles do not merely protect self-government as such. (I think that Post would agree.) To be sure, self-government is a defining value, perhaps the core value, but the classic First Amendment principles go far beyond that.[34] They protect novelists, poets, singers, artists, and actors. They also protect students, faculty, and administrators, even against their own (public) universities. The proof, of course, is in the pudding. We'll get to that.

Unsettled Questions

The final general point is that in some respects, the law here is quite underdeveloped. The Supreme Court has said a great deal, of course, about what federal and state governments may do with respect to speech, and it has offered a series of informative decisions on what secondary schools may do.[35] The Court has said that such schools are "nurseries of democracy," and hence must protect a great deal of speech, including off-campus speech.[36] Even so, secondary schools have considerable room to maneuver, precisely because they are secondary schools, and they are generally dealing with minors.[37] By contrast, there is not a great deal of law on what colleges and universities may do.[38] Universities are not nurseries, which means that they have less room to regulate speech than secondary schools do.

In an important passage from decades ago, the Court spoke broadly in favor of the full application of standard free speech principles to college campuses: "[T]he precedents of this Court leave no room for the view that, because of the acknowledged need for order, First Amendment protections should apply with less force on college campuses than in the community at large."[39] But that statement cannot possibly be read literally. "First Amendment protections" do not allow the government to prevent people from discussing politics on the street, but they do allow universities to prevent teachers and students from discussing Taylor Swift during biology class. "First Amendment protections" forbid the government from banning the use of obscenities in courthouses, but they may not forbid universities from banning the use of certain four-letter words in classrooms.[40] "First Amendment protections" do not allow the government to ban the making of sexually explicit videos (so long as they are not obscene), but they may not forbid universities from banning their president or chancellor from making sexually explicit videos. There are many unsettled questions.

Still, most actual and imaginable questions have straightforward answers. Where the law is less than entirely clear, it is nonetheless possible to offer informed judgments about its likely content. It is true that in some cases, any such judgments must be tentative.

Let us now explore the details, dividing the scenarios into two categories: speech by students and speech by professors. As we shall see, the two raise somewhat different considerations. Some of the cases are variations on what has actually happened; some of them are hypothetical. As we shall also see, the goal here is to provide breadth, in the form of a tour of the horizon, rather than depth, in the form of full answers to the hardest questions. Some of the questions can be essentially resolved with brisk answers. But for some of them, a brisk answer is inadequate; I signal that fact where it is relevant. Some of the questions are very hard, and my answers to those questions are meant to be tentative.

Here we go.

· 2 ·

Students

1

Students make a public protest, on campus, of an ongoing war effort in which American soldiers and American resources have been engaged. During the protest, the students describe American officials as "brutal warmongers" bent on "killing innocent people." The university believes that the protest is "disruptive, disrespectful, and unpatriotic" and "inconsistent with love of country." For that reason, it wants to ban the protest and punish the students.

This is an easy case. The university cannot ban the protest or punish the students. On the facts as stated, any such action would almost certainly be viewpoint-based.[1] The university cannot plausibly justify any such ban or punishment by reference to its educational mission.[2] (A time, place, and manner restriction would raise different questions.[3])

2

A group of students calling themselves "the Putin brigade" marches in a university quadrangle in support of Russia, saying, in slogans, that the Russian military action in Ukraine is justified to combat "NATO expansionism" and "US imperialism." Another group of students stages a counterprotest in support of Ukraine, describing Russia as "authoritarian aggressors" and "Nazis." Members of the second group shout at members of the first, using incendiary language.

On the facts as stated, the university cannot punish either side. It can prevent violence, and it can act if the *Brandenburg* test is met, but it cannot prevent the two groups from marching and speaking (or shouting).[4] Things would, of course, be different if violence actually breaks out. Universities are allowed to prevent violence. And as in case 1, things might be different if the university invoked a time, place, and manner restriction.

3

Members of a student group called Students for Palestine march through campus, saying over and over again, "Intifada now, intifada tomorrow, intifada forever."

The speech is highly likely to be protected by the First Amendment. The word "intifada" means "uprising" or "rebellion."[5] It appears to mean, in context, that a civil uprising would be appropriate in Palestine. A claim to that effect cannot be punished. The case is very close to the student protest at issue in case 1. It might be tempting to insist that some people would understand the group's words to suggest something different from a civil uprising (say, the destruction of Israel). But under existing law, what matters is what the speakers intend—whether their speech is "directed to inciting"—not what the audience hears.[6] In any case, an argument on behalf of violence is not regulable as such. Indeed, a lower court found that the First Amendment protected a planned march by Nazis in Skokie, Illinois, even though Skokie had a large Jewish population, including several thousand survivors of the Holocaust.[7] Recall the *Brandenburg* test.

The reason the speech is "highly likely to be" protected, and not definitely protected, is that there might be an argument that the march is intended to produce and likely to produce imminent lawless action.[8] On the facts as stated, that does not seem to be an easy argument to make, but we could recast the facts to make the argument more plausible. Nor is the university's educational mission a sufficient justification for regulating the speech; see case 1.

As in case 1, different questions would arise if the university were imposing a time, place, and manner restriction.

4

Same as case 3, but this time the student group also loudly calls for "the destruction of Israel." It believes, and says, that Israel should not have been created in the first place, and that it should be destroyed now.

This is less straightforward than case 3. The relevant speech calls for the destruction, by force, of a nation, and it might have negative effects on the university community by virtue of the fear that it might inculcate in some of the community's members. Nonetheless, the speech is probably protected. There is no direct threat against any members of the community. As the case is described, we cannot say that the speech was directed to produce and is likely to produce imminent lawless action. Recall that there is no general "incitement exception" to the First Amendment. Here once more, a time, place, and manner restriction would raise different questions.

5

Students for a Palestinian State, a group on campus, plans on show-ing a film called *The Occupation*. The film portrays Israel in an ex-ceedingly negative light—as a brutal, savage, occupying nation. It makes comparisons between Israel and Nazi Germany. It calls Israe-lis "the new Nazis."

In all likelihood, the university cannot ban the film or punish students for showing it.[9] The First Amendment protects students who want to show the film. Yet again, the case would be different if the film could be seen as directed to incite and likely to incite im-minent lawless action.[10] It might also be different if the university had some viewpoint-neutral policy in place that would be violated by a showing of the film. But if such a policy were content-based (for example, "no films or documentaries on the conflict in the Middle East"), it would be difficult to defend.[11]

6

A group of students has organized themselves as Students for a Christian America. They hold meetings, distribute pamphlets, and circulate a newsletter in which they say that "the United States is a Christian nation" and add that "non-Christians do not belong here." The university wants to discipline the students.

This is not a hard case. The statements in the newsletter cannot easily be interpreted as intending to incite, and likely to incite, imminent lawless action.[12] Unless they can be, the university cannot punish the relevant students. If it did so, it would likely be acting in a viewpoint-based way, and it could not readily justify its action on the grounds that it is essential to its educational mission. To be sure, it might try to do that, arguing that the relevant statements make some members of its community feel demeaned, unwanted, and at risk. But under current constitutional standards, that is not enough.

7

A group of students says to another student, whom they despise: "If we run across you in a secluded space, you're toast. We don't want your type around here."

The students have issued a "true threat," which is not protected by the First Amendment.[13] If someone threatens violence against another person, they lose their constitutional shield. At least this is true if the people who spoke the relevant words knew that there was a substantial risk that their communications would be taken to threaten violence.[14] In the case we are considering, the students certainly knew that, which means that they can be punished. It does not matter whether the threat was a product of personal animus, racial animus, religious animus, or something else.

8

A group of students issues a warning to Hispanic students, whom they despise: "If we run across any of you in a secluded space, you're toast. We don't want your type around here." The statement is a broad one, directed not to any particular Hispanic student, but to Hispanic students in general.

Same result as case 7. Here as well, the students have issued a true threat, which is not protected by the First Amendment. It does not matter that the threat is directed against a group of students rather than one or two.

9

Students engage in a protest of same-sex marriage, which, in their view, is "a desecration of marriage." They believe, and say, that "homosexuality is a sin" and that "homosexuals are sick in the head." The university forbids the protest on the grounds that it is "disrespectful to the law of the land and the United States Constitution" and "inconsistent with the university's defining values of diversity, equity, and inclusion."

This is a relatively easy case. The university has violated the First Amendment. It appears to have acted in a viewpoint-based way, and it cannot plausibly justify its action by reference to its educational mission.[15] The best argument that it can make would invoke that mission: the university might say that it is trying to protect LGBTQ students from feeling threatened, at risk, humiliated, or excluded from the community, and that it restricts any speech that has such an effect on any group. But that argument cuts too broadly. It would prevent students and faculty from expressing a point of view on many publicly contested issues. Under existing law, this kind of viewpoint discrimination cannot be plausibly defended.

10

Students engage in a protest of same-sex marriage, which, in their view, is "a desecration of marriage." They believe, and say, that "homosexuality is a sin." As part of their protest, they target individual students whom they believe to be gay or lesbian, approaching them in the halls and asking them "to find the right path." The university tells the students to stop doing what they are doing.

To evaluate this situation, we need to know what the targeting specifically entails. If it can be seen as a true threat—that is, if the protesters "consciously disregarded a substantial risk that [their] communications would be viewed as threatening violence"[16]—it can of course be regulated. If there is no such threat, but instead a form of personal engagement with particular students that verges on or constitutes bullying, the question is harder.[17] There is no *general* "bullying" or "harassment" exception to the First Amendment, but under current law, certain forms of bullying (including certain forms of cyberbullying) and harassment appear to be unprotected.[18] Those kinds of bullying and harassment can be punished on campus, at least if they are suitably defined.

It is difficult to deal with this scenario without specifying the kind of conduct and the degree of invasiveness that are involved. This area of law continues to evolve, but a key question is whether the protesters are targeting individuals, as individuals, in a way that makes them feel at some kind of personal risk. If the targeting is an effort at persuasion, akin to an aggressive political campaign, an attempt at religious conversion, or a charitable solicitation, it cannot be regulated. As the scenario is described, it seems more like an effort at persuasion, which means that the relevant speech is protected.

11

A group of students decides to have a "white pride" week. During that week, they hold daily events celebrating "the many achievements of white people" and deploring "constant efforts to make white people ashamed of themselves." The university would like to punish the students.

This is not a hard case. The students cannot be punished. Some members of the university community will be offended, outraged, or worse by the relevant events, but the First Amendment does not allow any kind of punishment.[19] To be sure, the university might argue that the whole idea of a white pride week is fatally inconsistent with its educational mission, because it would make many members of its community feel disparaged and unwelcome. But even in the university setting, the First Amendment does not allow speech to be regulated because people would feel disparaged and unwelcome. Speech in favor of white pride does not fall within a regulable category, even if it is correctly taken, by many or most, to be full of ugly or horrific implications and resonances.

12

Same as case 11, but the students also say that "white people are more intelligent than people of color" and that "people of color are more prone to violence than white people." They march and chant, "White is Beautiful" and "White is Best." The university would like to punish the students.

This case is harder than case 11, simply because it goes far beyond a statement in favor of white pride. The university might argue that speech of this kind is threatening to students of color, might be directed at producing imminent lawless action, and is inconsistent with its educational mission. It might spell out that argument by saying that the relevant speech would make reasonable students (and faculty) feel disparaged or unwelcome on campus. Pause, if you would, over exactly what is being said, and over its likely meaning in light of American history.

Fair enough. But on the facts as stated, no individual students are being threatened or singled out; we do not have a "true treat" as the Supreme Court understands it. There is no "hate speech" exception to the First Amendment. The educational mission is not a license for restrictions on speech that is offensive, insulting, demeaning, or even in some general sense threatening. Under existing law, some bullets need to be bitten: the speech is likely to be protected. Unless the *Brandenburg* test is met, this is a case for use of, and insistence on, counterspeech and governing norms rather than sanctions.

One qualification: I am attempting, here as throughout, to channel existing First Amendment law, but because the speech is occurring in the university setting, we are not dealing with a simple case, or one on which reasonable people might not differ. In particular, those who emphasize the university's educational mission might insist that the statements in this case endanger that mission, especially if they are repeated, because of their severely corrosive effects on members of the community. The argument is unlikely to succeed under current law, but it is not a self-evident loser. There is also a possibility that in cases of this kind, some private universities would choose not to follow the First Amendment, which, it will be recalled, does not bind them (on this issue, see Chapter 4).

13

Same as case 12, but the week is not "white pride week," it is "white supremacy week."[20] All of its events are organized around the theme of white supremacy. The university would like to punish the students.

This case can be seen as even harder than case 12. The idea of white supremacy has its own history (and its own present). In that light, the university might credibly argue that speech of this kind is threatening to students of color, is directed at producing imminent lawless action, and (in particular) is inconsistent with its educational mission. The latter point in particular might be spelled out in considerable detail, and it might be made quite forceful. But it remains relevant that on these facts, again, no individual students are threatened or singled out. We need to know more about the details and the risk of lawless action, but under existing law in general and *Brandenburg* in particular, the speech is likely to be protected. To that extent, the right answer is again counterspeech and norms, not punishment.

In this case, and perhaps in case 12, the university might also invoke *Beauharnais v. Illinois*, decided in 1952, where the Court upheld a statute saying:

> It shall be unlawful for any person, firm or corporation to manufacture, sell, or offer for sale, advertise or publish, present or exhibit in any public place in this state any lithograph, moving picture, play, drama or sketch, which publication or exhibition portrays depravity, criminality, unchastity, or lack of virtue of a class of citizens, of any race, color, creed or religion which said publication or exhibition exposes the citizens of any race, color, creed or religion to contempt, derision, or obloquy or which is productive of breach of the peace or riots. . . . [21]

In explaining why that statute was valid, the Court pointed to the historical legitimation of libel laws and said that "if an utterance directed at an individual may be the object of criminal sanctions, we cannot deny to a State power to punish the same utterance directed at a defined group unless we can say that this is a willful and purposeless restriction unrelated to the peace and wellbeing of the State."[22] But *Beauharnais* does not seem to be good law. In *New York Times v. Sullivan,* of course, the Court imposed severe restrictions on use of libel law.[23] In addition, *R.A.V. v. City of St. Paul* held that viewpoint discrimination is impermissible even within the category of unprotected speech.[24]

In light of these decisions, it is generally assumed that *Beauharnais* is a dead letter. If that assumption turns out to be wrong, or if it is wrong in the context of campus speech, we could imagine a variation on case 13, or perhaps case 13 itself, being resolved in a way that allows the university to impose regulation. And as we have seen, cases 12 and 13 are not all that easy even if *Beauharnais* is indeed dead, because of a not implausible argument about the university's educational mission. It remains true that under existing law, that argument is unlikely to succeed.

14

In an essay about the assassination of Abraham Lincoln, a student "borrows" several paragraphs from a book on the topic, without attribution. Claiming that this is a case of plagiarism, the professor gives the student a failing grade and refers the student for disciplinary proceedings. The student is suspended.

There is no constitutional problem. Students do not have a constitutional right to plagiarize.

15

A student uses ChatGPT to write a term paper in an English course. The university forbids students from using ChatGPT and other large language models (LLMs) to write term papers. The student insists that he has a right to use whatever sources might be helpful.

The university can punish the student. Just as there is no constitutional right to engage in plagiarism, so there is no constitutional right to use LLMs to write a term paper. This is so even if some prohibitions on use of LLMs (for example, viewpoint-based restrictions) would raise serious constitutional problems.[25]

16

A student submits a twenty-page paper on Samuel Beckett's *Waiting for Godot* for her literature course. The student had a hard time getting started, so she consulted ChatGPT and asked it to write the opening paragraphs. After it did so, she was able to write her paper. She revised the opening paragraphs significantly, so that they count, in her view, as her own work.

The professor notices that the opening paragraphs are written in a somewhat different style from the rest of the paper, and asks the student what happened. She provides an honest account. The professor gives her a very low grade in the class, noting that under university policy, she is not permitted to use LLMs even for this limited purpose.

Any kind of punishment might seem harsh in this context, but there is no First Amendment problem. A university can impose a flat ban on the use of AI tools if it wishes.

17

A university forbids the use of university technology, including university email, to cause "offense to others" or "embarrassment to the university." A group of students believes that the prohibition is so open-ended that it is unacceptably vague. They add that they are deterred from using the university's email system for fear that their words will be deemed to be in violation of the prohibition.

The university's policy violates the First and Fourteenth Amendments. It is indeed unconstitutionally vague. It does not give fair notice to reasonable people trying to figure out what is permitted and what is prohibited.[26] The university's policy is also overbroad. It forbids a lot of speech that is protected by the First Amendment.

18

A speaker has been invited to give a talk on "the threat of immigration" at a public university The speaker believes that immigration is "destroying America" and "must be stopped." Students protest the speaker, shouting him down and preventing him from giving his remarks.

The students can be punished. There is no First Amendment right to shout down speakers.[27]

19

Students occupy a university building and block access to it. They do so on the grounds that the university is "complicit" in horrific national policies. They argue that because the university has refused to "take a stand" against those policies, it is rightly subject to this form of protest, until and unless it "decides it has to change."

The students can be stopped and punished. There is no First Amendment right to occupy and block access to a building.[28]

20

Students stand outside a building, protesting a university's silence on a matter of public concern. A large group is assembled. The leaders argue that the group should "storm the building" and "take it over for a week, maybe more," to make their views "clear and heard."

There is a very strong argument that the students can be stopped and punished. It appears that their words are directed to incite and likely to incite imminent lawless action.[29]

21

Students occupy a common room at a university. They do so on the grounds that the university is "complicit" in horrific national policies. They argue that because the university has refused to "take a stand" against those policies, it is rightly subject to this form of

protest, unless and until it "decides it has to change." While they occupy the room, they do not block access to it, and they do not take
up all the seats; the room is still available for some students to use.

On the facts as stated, the students can probably be punished.
Suppose that the university has a viewpoint-neutral policy, stating
that the common room is a "place for quiet study and contempla-
tion," and forbidding public expressive activities of any kind in that
place. If so, the policy is in the nature of a time, place, and manner
restriction, subject to a balancing test (see Chapter 1).[30] To the extent that the occupation of the common room allows only a small
number of students to use it, the case for upholding the restriction
is very strong. Even if the disruption is minimal, there continues to
be a good argument that the university should be allowed to dedi-
cate certain spaces for certain purposes. Of course, the question
would be harder if the university engaged in content discrimination, forbidding political activities but allowing, say, religious or
purely educational activities. This would be a subject matter restriction, which is a form of content discrimination.

22

A law school dean holds a social gathering at his private home for
law students, celebrating the end of the semester. Students who
have been invited to the gathering decide to hold a political protest,
condemning certain decisions, real or imagined, of the dean, the
law school, and the university.[31] The dean tells the students to leave
on the grounds that they were invited for a social occasion, not a

protest. The students refuse to do so. The law school suspends the students for a semester.

The suspension does not offend the First Amendment. There is no constitutional right to protest on private property. No one has a right to engage in trespass for protest activity. The case might be thought to be a bit harder because the students had been invited onto the property, but after they disrupted the occasion, were asked to leave, and refused to do so, they became trespassers. The First Amendment does not shield trespassers.[32]

23

A number of student groups are deeply alarmed by what they see as horrific actions by the government of Israel in the aftermath of the terrorist attacks by Hamas on October 7, 2023. They engage in protest activities at a large university.[33] Their protest activities are in violation of the university's rules about how to use campus spaces. Among other things, those rules forbid students from setting up tents in such spaces, require students to identify themselves upon request, prohibit students from damaging campus property, and ban students from interfering with the operations of the university. Because the students have violated the university's rules, they have been suspended and are no longer welcome on campus. They are considered to be trespassers and are subject to arrest. Some of them are arrested.

The initial question is whether the university's rules are consistent with the First Amendment. They are plainly content-neutral.

Indeed, they are something we have not seen before: *incidental restrictions on speech*. A speed limit law, for example, does not target speech; it is designed to produce safe driving. If someone violates the speed limit law in order to protest speed limit laws, they cannot claim the benefit of the First Amendment. A protester might want to trespass on the property of a company that makes gas-powered cars as a way of protesting climate change, but if the law forbids people from trespassing on private property (and it does), the incidental effect on speech does not give them any kind of safe harbor. A protester might want to steal an expensive car to protest inequality, but the First Amendment does not protect thieves.

The leading Supreme Court case on incidental restrictions on speech involved a congressional prohibition on the destruction or mutilation of Selective Service registration certificates, more commonly known as "draft cards."[34] David Paul O'Brien, along with three companions, burned his registration certificate as part of a protest against the Vietnam War. The Supreme Court said that the law that O'Brien violated was an "incidental" limitation on free speech, and that "a sufficiently important governmental interest in regulating the nonspeech element can justify" such a limitation. The Court added that "a government regulation is sufficiently justified if it is within the constitutional power of the Government; if it furthers an important or substantial governmental interest; if the governmental interest is unrelated to the suppression of free expression, and if the incidental restriction on alleged First Amendment freedoms is no greater than is essential to the furtherance of that interest."[35]

That's a mouthful. The basic idea is that if a law that incidentally punishes speech, or protest, is designed to protect a legitimate interest, it is almost certainly going to be upheld. In practice, the test for incidental restrictions on speech is more lenient than the test for content-neutral restrictions on speech.

In this light, the university's rules would be exceedingly difficult to challenge. It is clearly legitimate to protect campus property, and the same is true of university operations. (We might worry about vagueness, but let's bracket that for now.) The requirement that students identify themselves is an effort to ensure against trespass. That, too, is legitimate. A prohibition on the construction of tents is not directed against speech; it is directed against tents. In all likelihood, the university could urge that its ordinary operations, in the relevant places, would be disrupted if tents were established there. A university is entitled to say that students cannot put up tents, or put down sleeping bags, on campus. Under existing law, the incidental restriction on speech does not offend the Constitution.

What about suspending the students? What about arresting them? Reasonable people might disagree about whether those steps are too harsh, but there is no First Amendment problem. Trespassers can be suspended or arrested.

24

Students start a new organization: Christians for Christianity. They say that "all students are welcome to join," so long as they are willing to accept the principles of the organization. The university is deeply troubled. It does not want to ban the new organization, but it does not want to give it the kind of financial support that it normally gives to student organizations. It says that funding of religious organizations is uniquely divisive, and hence refuses to fund the new organization.

The university has violated the First Amendment. It has discriminated on the basis of viewpoint.[36]

25

Members of a student group called Students for Socialism have decided that during class they will not address the topics assigned by the teacher, but will speak only about the importance of, and the need for, socialism in the United States. In response to questions about biology or literature, they explain why they are committed to socialism.

The students may be punished, so long as they are not being discriminated against on the basis of viewpoint. To promote its educational mission, a university may insist on a simple proposition: class time is for class.[37] This conclusion is broadly consistent with *Pickering* and *Connick*.

26

A student uses profanity in a political science class, including the words *fuck* and *shit*. The university forbids the use of profanity in class, under a clearly stated policy. The official goal of the policy is to ensure discussions that are "respectful" and "civil."

Whether the student may be punished is not an easy question. The Supreme Court has made it clear that profanity might be protected even if it occurs in special environments, such as courtrooms.[38] Following the Court's holding in *Cohen v. California*, a university is generally not permitted to forbid the use of obscenities outside of the classroom.[39] But inside the classroom, it might plausibly say that it is trying to maintain a certain kind of tone, one that is conducive to learning. For high schools, the Court has said something like this with respect to speech before a school assembly.[40] In particular, the Court said:

> The undoubted freedom to advocate unpopular and controversial views in schools and classrooms must be balanced against the society's countervailing interest in teaching students the boundaries of socially appropriate behavior. Even the most heated political discourse in a democratic society requires consideration for the personal sensibilities of the other participants and audiences.[41]

In refusing to protect the use of profanity, the Court emphasized that it was dealing with "children in a public school." In a paragraph that fits with the general approach in *Pickering*, the Court referred to the educational mission:

> The process of educating our youth for citizenship in public schools is not confined to books, the curriculum, and the civics class; schools must teach by example the shared

values of a civilized social order. Consciously or otherwise, teachers—and indeed the older students—demonstrate the appropriate form of civil discourse and political expression by their conduct and deportment in and out of class. Inescapably, like parents, they are role models. The schools, as instruments of the state, may determine that the essential lessons of civil, mature conduct cannot be conveyed in a school that tolerates lewd, indecent, or offensive speech and conduct.[42]

Might these ideas apply to the university? That is not at all clear. University students are not children. Still, it is not unreasonable to say that frequent or constant use of obscenities in a university class may severely compromise the educational mission. But punishment for a onetime use, or an exuberant or infrequent use, might raise a serious constitutional issue.

27

A group of students is outraged by the behavior of the police in major cities across the United States. The group puts together a cartoon, "The Real America," in which police officers are depicted as gang-raping the Statue of Liberty. The university suspends the students.

The suspension is unconstitutional under the *Papish* case, a ruling from 1973.[43] The speech is not obscene in the sense in which the Supreme Court understands the idea of obscenity. The university is discriminating on the basis of content, and probably of viewpoint as well. Still, it is possible that the current Supreme Court would revisit the 1973 ruling. As Chief Justice Burger wrote in his dissenting opinion:

> In theory, at least, a university is not merely an arena for the discussion of ideas by students and faculty; it is also an institution where individuals learn to express themselves in acceptable, civil terms. We provide that environment to the end that students may learn the self-restraint necessary to the functioning of a civilized society and understand the need for those external restraints to which we must all submit if group existence is to be tolerable.[44]

I have said a few things about this way of thinking, and I will return to it below in the context of faculty speech. But under the law as it now stands, no university can discipline a student for writing and publishing such a cartoon.

28

Students form an organization called the Real America Society. The organization is devoted to "traditional values," which include "God, Country, and Family, in that order." Members of the organization believe that "America has lost its way," that "woke is a mental illness," that "diversity, equity, and inclusion is a disgrace," that "men and women are different by nature," and that "modern civil rights laws intrude on freedom." The university denies funding for the organization, on the grounds that resources are limited and should not be given to a group that "would offend the basic dignity of members of our community." The university does so even though it generally funds any and all student organizations; it does not run a competitive process.

The denial of funding is probably unconstitutional under the Supreme Court's decision in *Rosenberger*.[45] In that case, the Court ruled that the University of Virginia could not deny funding to an organization whose student newspaper, *Wide Awake: A Christian Perspective at the University of Virginia,* promoted a particular set of religious beliefs. The Court emphasized that viewpoint discrimination is generally impermissible. On that point, it spoke broadly: "If the topic of debate is, for example, racism, then exclusion of several views on that problem is just as offensive to the First Amendment as exclusion of only one. It is as objectionable to exclude both a theistic and an atheistic perspective on the debate as it is to exclude one, the other, or yet another political, economic, or social viewpoint."[46] And in fact, the relevant principles have particular force in the university setting: "For the University, by regulation, to cast disapproval on particular viewpoints of its students risks the suppression of free speech and creative inquiry in one of the vital centers for the Nation's intellectual life, its college and university campuses."[47]

The limits of *Rosenberger* are not altogether clear.[48] The Court did not say that viewpoint-neutral, content-based funding decisions are unacceptable. That would be preposterous; for funding, content-based decisions may turn out to be *inevitable,* at least if a university has more applicants than it can fund and does not run a lottery. But in the scenario described here, which appears to involve viewpoint discrimination, it seems evident that *Rosenberger* controls.

The strongest argument by the university would point to its educational mission. The university might argue that viewpoint discrimination cannot always be prohibited in the funding context. This is an unresolved question. What about the Society for the Murder of Jews, the Society Dedicated to Rape, or the Society for the Restoration of Slavery? In the educational setting, some such organizations might be deemed beyond the pale, because they are so clearly inconsistent with the university's core values or its central mission. But the Real America Society is not like those organizations. In any case, specification of the relevant line, if there even is one, is not at all straightforward. If an organization is specifically created in order to promote unlawful behavior, perhaps the university can probably deny funding to it, even if it could not suppress the relevant speech.[49] The *Brandenburg* test might support that conclusion, and even if the test is not met, it seems eminently reasonable to suggest that a university need not fund an organization whose purpose is to promote crime. After all, conspiracies are not protected by the First Amendment.

· 3 ·

Professors

1

A professor publishes an online essay in which she says that "the sex police are working overtime," that "diversity, inclusion, and equity have gone fascist," and that "political correctness is completely out of control." Among other things, she argues that rules against romantic relationships between professors and students are "draconian" and "appalling," because they ignore "what we know about the complexity, the mystery, and the sheer wonder of desire."

This is an easy case. The professor cannot be punished. What she has said does not fall within any category of unprotected speech. The university might argue that a professor who has written such things cannot perform the duties of a professor, because some students might feel "vulnerable" or "unsafe" in her class. But on the facts as stated, this argument is difficult to make. Nothing in the online essay represents a threat or harassment, or anything close to it.[1] A physical threat or harassment is one thing; what some students might see as wrongheaded, offensive, or worse is another. To be sure, many students will have an intensely negative reaction.

But as Justice Oliver Wendell Holmes Jr. said, the First Amendment protects "freedom for the thought we hate."[2]

2

A professor writes an op-ed in which she claims that Islam is "a violent religion," that Muslims are "prone to violence," and that "Christianity is the religion of peace." She writes that "Islamic terrorism has ancient roots." Many of her colleagues and students are deeply offended. The university suspends her for a semester, saying, "This kind of hatred and stereotyping does not belong in our community."

The suspension violates the First Amendment. This is content discrimination and probably viewpoint discrimination as well.[3] The university's best argument would be that the op-ed in question makes it hard for the professor to teach her classes; might Muslim students feel unwelcome? Maybe so. The problem is that the argument would have unacceptably broad consequences for speech by professors outside of class. On the facts as stated, it is insufficient to support a suspension. There is no evidence that the professor has discriminated against Muslim students in class, or that her views have had any effect on her teaching.

3

A professor of psychology writes an article claiming that climate change is not real. The paper argues that the science underlying current concerns is "built on sand" and that people believe in climate change largely because of certain psychological biases, including the availability heuristic and the representativeness heuristic. He also argues that belief in climate change has become "the official religion of the far left."

The First Amendment almost certainly protects the professor against any kind of reprisal.[4] The reason for the qualification ("almost certainly") is that if the article is shoddy and does not live up to professional standards, the university might be able to say that any reprisal is viewpoint-neutral. Under the circumstances as described, however, that does not appear to be likely.

4

An assistant professor of English literature writes a series of papers condemning "capitalism" on the grounds that it is a "recipe for both poverty and war." The papers fall well below professional standards. The university does not promote the assistant professor.

To know whether the university's decision violates the First Amendment, we need to know more. A viewpoint-based action on the university's part might well be forbidden. But suppose that the professor is not being promoted only because many of his papers fall below professional standards.[5] A policy to that effect is unobjectionable. Of course that policy would be content-based, but judgments about hiring, retention, and tenure are inevitably content-based, at least in the sense that work must be assessed on the basis of what it says. A professor whose work is shoddy need not be promoted.

5

A history professor teaching a course on the Civil War decides to spend a class explaining why he favors one presidential candidate over another. He connects his preference to what he sees as the arc of American history, but he does not relate his comments to the Civil War.

This is an easy case. The professor can be punished, so long as the university is acting in a viewpoint-neutral fashion. Suppose, for example, that the university has adopted a principle requiring teachers to focus on the subject of their courses and not to depart from that subject to elaborate their political views during classroom hours. A content-based, viewpoint-neutral principle of this kind can be justified as essential to the university's educational mission.[6] *Pickering* and *Connick* suggest that the university can do as it reasonably wishes here.[7] The case would be much harder for the university if the professor merely stated his political views briefly or casually, or in the ordinary course of teaching the subject. The case would also be much harder for the university if there is even a whiff of viewpoint discrimination.

6

A professor uses social media to criticize his university's policies with respect to diversity, equity, and inclusion (DEI), and also to say that affirmative action is "an insult to everyone, including those it supposedly benefits." He repeatedly casts contempt on DEI initiatives and says that they should be "abolished immediately." The university tells him that he has "crossed the line" and threatens to remove him from a leadership position in his department (which comes with a $15,000 stipend).

At first glance, the case is straightforward: the university has acted unconstitutionally. The professor's speech does not fall in any unprotected category, and the university's educational mission does not mean that it can insulate itself from serious criticism. The strongest response, based on *Pickering,* would be that a leader of a department cannot publicly disparage policies that he is charged with implementing.[8] We might need to know more about the leadership position to come to terms with this response. But the university would have a steep hill to climb. It is hardly impossible for a leader to act responsibly in his position even if he is on record as vigorously opposing some of his institution's policies.

7

A professor is exceedingly harsh with his students. He repeatedly tells them that they are "stupid," "hopeless," and "incompetent." The students report that they are demoralized and "cannot learn" in the face of their teacher's harshness.

The professor can be punished for speech of this kind. A general prohibition on exceedingly harsh interactions with students is viewpoint-neutral, and it is reasonably justified as essential to the university's educational mission (though there might be a question of vagueness, if the relevant policy does not give fair notice[9]).

Here, too, *Pickering* and *Connick* suggest that the university can do as it reasonably wishes.[10]

8

A professor uses various epithets in class, directed at women, Jews, Hispanics, and Blacks. He says that he wants his students "to develop a thick skin."

The professor can be punished. The teacher is acting in a generally abusive way, with the abuse directed at individual students. That kind of abuse is not protected in the educational setting, certainly not when a professor is the abuser. Consistent with *Pickering* and *Connick,* a university can reasonably conclude that abuse of this kind is patently inconsistent with its educational mission.[11]

9

A professor uses the word *n---er* in class. She does so not to insult anyone, but as part of a set of hypothetical questions testing the limits of freedom of speech. Many students are offended, appalled, or both. She says: "That's part of my point!"

This case is not entirely easy, but in the end, it is not hard. The best answer is that the professor cannot be punished. The reason that it is not entirely easy is that the "n-word" has a unique history, and a university might reasonably believe that its use has a distinct and damaging effect on the educational environment. But at least in the case under discussion, where no individual is being targeted and the use of the word is connected to the subject matter of the particular class, this content-based restriction on speech is difficult to defend as essential to the educational mission.[12] That is why the case is not hard.

10

A professor says, in class, that if he did not allow students to use the internet in class, he would be "lynched." Students of color are offended by the reference and ask the university to punish the professor.

This is an easy case. Any such punishment would offend the First Amendment. The use of the word "lynched" in this context may be ill-considered, but it does not plausibly fall within any category of unprotected speech.

11

A white professor wears blackface at a Halloween party. He says that he is doing so "because it's politically incorrect!" and "to get people to laugh a little," and "because it's not woke." He thinks that people should "lighten up—no pun intended."

The professor cannot be punished. He has almost certainly offended people, but he has not engaged in speech that falls in any unprotected category.[13] The university might argue that he has acted in a way that compromises the educational mission, but that would prove too much. If any offense compromises the educational mission, the constitutional rights of professors begin to evaporate; free speech is gone.

12

A faculty member sexually harasses a student. He does not merely ask for a romantic relationship; he signals that if she agrees to such a relationship, he will help her professionally. He says, "It would be really good for your career if you slept with me."

The faculty member can be punished. Sexual harassment of this kind is not protected by the First Amendment.[14] It is akin to uttering the words "you are fired" to discharge someone on the basis of race, sex, or religion. Note that it would probably not be useful to say, in cases of this kind, that we are dealing with conduct rather than speech.[15] We are dealing with speech, and the relevant speech is not protected.

13

A professor repeatedly compliments a student's appearance and asks her on dates. She declines his advances and asks him to stop. He does not stop.

The professor can be punished. Sexual harassment of this kind is not protected by the First Amendment.[16]

14

A male professor makes a series of sexually charged comments in class. He says, "I don't know what the admissions office is up to these days, but the women here are looking more beautiful than ever." He adds, "Looking at the women here, it's hard to teach; I am pretty distracted." He says, "I'm certainly glad that I'm married. Otherwise I might say or do something I would regret."

The professor can be punished. Here as well, sexual harassment of this kind is not protected by the First Amendment. More precisely, these comments might count as "hostile environment" sexual harassment, and the First Amendment does not forbid a university from punishing them as such. Even if they do not meet the bar for sexual harassment in the technical sense, a university can say, without offense to the First Amendment, that such comments are inconsistent with its educational mission.

We can imagine a harder case involving an isolated statement or "microaggression." Suppose, for example, that a male professor says, in class, "I think women are amazing," or "If I am going to dinner at someone's house, I hope the wife is cooking, not the husband," or "Women's sports just don't impress me," or "Men are stronger than women, but women have more emotional intelligence." It would be extreme to punish a professor for making statements of this kind. Here again, we have a situation where relying on norms, and not sanctions, is the appropriate response. Are such statements protected by the First Amendment? There is a strong argument that they are, especially if an effort to punish someone for making them is viewpoint-based. A pattern of making such statements would present a different question; such a pattern might create a hostile environment, and it might be the basis for a reprimand, or more, in response to a series of inappropriate and irrelevant comments in class, damaging to the educational mission.

15

Same as case 12, 13, or 14, but the professor is female. Same conclusion. It does not matter whether the professor is male or female. It does not matter whether a male professor is harassing female students, a female professor is harassing male students, a male professor is harassing male students, or a female professor is harassing female students.

16

A university committee, consisting of both administrators and professors, decides to remove certain books from the university library. It does so on the grounds that the relevant books are "inconsistent with American values," "un-Christian," and "just plain dirty." A group of professors and students objects on constitutional grounds.

We need to know the details, but the removal might well be unconstitutional under the Supreme Court's decision in *Pico*.[17] In that case, based on similar facts, a plurality of the Court said that with respect to school libraries, "discretion may not be exercised in a narrowly partisan or political manner."[18] In short, the plurality said, "[o]ur Constitution does not permit the official suppression of *ideas*," which means that everything depends on the motivations of the authorities.[19] If those authorities "*intended* by their removal decision to deny . . . access to ideas with which [those authorities] disagreed, and if this intent was the decisive factor" in their decision, then the First Amendment has been violated.[20] At the same time, the plurality made it clear that authorities may remove books on the grounds that they are "vulgar" or that they do not meet standards of "educational suitability."[21] It follows that content discrimination is permissible in this domain, and possibly a form of viewpoint discrimination as well. Can decisions about "educational suitability" be made without considering viewpoint? That is a fair question.

In light of *Pico*, the removal at hand might well violate the First Amendment. We are dealing here with the official suppression of ideas, and the authorities seem to have intended to deny people access to ideas with which they disagreed. It must be noted, however, that the law here is not entirely stable. The plurality opinion was just that (four justices, not a majority of five), and while Justice Blackmun's concurring opinion was not substantially different ("I find crucial the State's decision to single out an idea for disapproval and then deny access to it"[22]), the ruling contains ambiguities, and five justices did not support the plurality's view. It must also be noted that there is no assurance that the current Court will or would accept the plurality's judgment in *Pico*. (For the record: I hope that it will.)

17

A university committee, consisting of both administrators and professors, decides on a new policy regarding which books to purchase for the university library. Under the new policy, the university will not purchase books that are "inconsistent with American values," "un-Christian," and "just plain dirty." A group of professors and students objects on constitutional grounds.

This case is harder than case 16. The reason is that universities do not have unlimited funds, and any decision about which books to buy must be selective. Choices must be made on the basis of content, and viewpoint discrimination is not impermissible. A university might decide that it is not going to buy books denying the existence of gravity, or celebrating Hitler and the Holocaust, or claiming that space aliens are among us and running our largest corporations. In view of the inevitability of content discrimination and viewpoint discrimination, it might be tempting to say that universities can do as they like, at least when they are deciding which books to buy.

We could put pressure on this conclusion. Suppose that a university decided to buy only books that are consistent with the views of one political party, or that praised, and did not criticize, recent presidents. We are in uncharted waters here, and there is no obvious resolution. The best approach might be to say that in deciding which books to purchase, universities have a great deal of room to maneuver, but that the First Amendment does not authorize the most egregious forms of political favoritism. If so, the policies described in the first paragraph above might well be struck down.

18

Same as case 16, but the decision to remove the books comes from a state legislature, not from the university. The analysis is identical. It does not matter whether the restriction comes from the university itself or from the relevant legislature.

19

In a course on race relations in the United States, a professor spends two classes on critical race theory, even though the university has banned the teaching of critical race theory.

This is not obviously a case that is not obvious, but it is indeed not an obvious case. On the one hand, the university can establish its own curriculum. It can insist that a course on race relations will focus on five specific books, and not on any other books. Indeed, the limits on viewpoint-based restrictions find their bounds here.[23] A university can insist that classes on evolution not include readings that question the idea of evolution, that courses on the Civil War not include readings that celebrate slavery, and that courses on astronomy not attend to the idea that the sun goes around the earth.

On the other hand, specific restrictions on specific points of view, rooted in political considerations rather than clear or even arguable pedagogical purposes, raise issues akin to those raised by removal of books from libraries.[24] Consider, for example, a university rule that no political science teacher may assign materials that speak ill of the current president or of leaders from a particular political party. Or imagine a university rule that no professor or student may "say anything negative about the United States or its traditions." Any such rule would be unconstitutional.

This is an area in which the line-drawing problem is formidable. A restriction on the communication of particular points of view would raise serious constitutional doubts.[25] But outside of the most egregious cases, in which viewpoint discrimination is un-mistakable and cannot be defended by reference to, say, scientific consensus, a university's establishment of a curriculum, and its de-cisions about what teachers may assign, should not be taken to run afoul of the First Amendment. Would a ban on teaching critical race theory count as an egregious case? I tend to think so.

20

A law school is hiring a new faculty member to teach constitutional law. There are two finalists for the position. One of them is an origi-nalist who calls for understanding the Constitution in accordance with its original public meaning, and she is quite conservative.[26] The other rejects originalism. She believes in moral readings of the Constitution, and she is left of center.[27] The faculty decides to hire the originalist. It does so in part on the grounds that she would add intellectual diversity to the institution, which has few conser-vatives and only one originalist among several dozen professors.

The law school has not violated the First Amendment. An insti-tution is allowed to pursue intellectual diversity. To be sure, there has been a degree of viewpoint discrimination here, but in this context, that form of discrimination is not invidious. A central goal of viewpoint discrimination, in this particular case, is to enlarge viewpoint diversity at the university as a whole.

We could imagine more difficult cases, in which, for example, people are not hired, or are denied tenure, because of opposition to their political convictions. To understand how to handle such cases, we need more details. Two considerations should orient the inquiry. On the one hand, not hiring people, or not giving people tenure, because of their convictions is a case of viewpoint discrimination. That raises a red flag. On the other hand, we need to know why, exactly, that discrimination is occurring. Is it to expand intellectual diversity in the community? Is it because some viewpoints (the earth is flat, Shakespeare was a capitalist stooge, Taylor Swift can't sing[28]) are beyond the pale, because they are demonstrably wrong or at least foolish?

In general, it would be very difficult for courts to police hiring decisions without running afoul of the interest in academic freedom. Imagine, for example, that a university decides not to hire someone whose research supports Nazism or Communism, and one of the reasons is antipathy to the relevant viewpoint. The university doesn't want Nazis or Communists on its faculty. Without resolving specific questions, some of which could be exceedingly hard, let us simply note that universities should be allowed a wide berth in such cases.

21

A university eliminates its comparative literature department. It does so on the grounds that "while the subject is important, student interest is low, and we want to use our resources for subjects that attract widespread student interest and that prepare students for a competitive marketplace."

The university has not violated the First Amendment. Nothing in the Constitution says that the decision whether to continue or to eliminate departments cannot depend on student interest or career preparation. There is content discrimination here, but it is not illicit, and there is no viewpoint discrimination.

22

A university discharges a tenured professor who teaches gender studies. It does so on the grounds that the new president and his team think that gender studies is "not a field," and that the professor "believes all sorts of preposterous things." (Let us bracket contractual issues; tenured professors have various protections, independent of the First Amendment.)

The discharge is almost certainly unconstitutional. There is a good argument that it is viewpoint-based.[29] It might even be part of some kind of "purge" of faculty members who depart from some kind of orthodoxy.

The reason for the term "almost certainly" is that we could imagine testing cases. Suppose that a university discharges a professor in its physics department on the grounds that he is spending all his time writing about visits with space aliens, or a professor in its English department on the grounds that she is devoting most of her class time to explaining why Shakespeare's plays were actually written by Jane Austen, or a professor in its history department on the grounds that he is writing a series of books on why World War II was actually started by Winston Churchill and Franklin Delano Roosevelt. Some apparently viewpoint-based actions, including disciplinary actions, are acceptable, at least if they are designed to ensure that professors do their job. Making demonstrably preposterous claims, in academic writing or in class, is a way of not doing their job.[30] To the extent possible, we should ensure that there are objective, and not political, grounds for identifying preposterous claims. Judges should be reluctant to second-guess a university's claims about what is preposterous. But in case 22, a little second-guessing does not seem out of bounds.

23

A university decides not to hire a professor who teaches gender studies. It does so on the grounds that the new president and his team think that gender studies is "not a field," and that the professor "believes all sorts of preposterous things."

This is significantly harder than case 22. A discharge is one thing; a failure to hire is another. A key reason is that a failure to hire might be based on a wide range of factors, and it will be difficult to show that viewpoint was the reason, or a but-for cause, of a failure to hire someone.[31] In any case, a university can certainly decide that it wants to hire someone who works on, say, elections, not someone who works on gender studies.[32] A university can also make decisions about which fields it values, or even considers to be fields. Indeed, universities must make such decisions in deciding whom to hire. Courts should and would tread lightly here. They might well adopt a very strong presumption against accepting free speech challenges to decisions about whom to hire.[33]

24

A university eliminates its gender studies department. It does so on the grounds that the new president and his team believe that the university's gender studies department "has become a place where students are taught preposterous, radical things," including that "gender is a social construction," that "there is no such thing as 'a woman,'" and that "the patriarchy is everywhere."

This is not an easy question. Actually, it is very tough. On the one hand, the elimination of the gender studies department is clearly viewpoint-based. We could imagine a purge of departments that officials do not like, because of the views that people in those departments express. A purge of individual faculty members who have disfavored views would clearly be unconstitutional; see case 22. Perhaps a purge of whole departments is similar.

On the other hand, we have seen that viewpoint discrimination is part and parcel of decisions about curriculum, departments, and offerings. A university can decide not to offer courses on the flatness of the earth, and it need not have a department on Nazi political science or Soviet biology.

To be sure, elimination of a department would raise different issues from a refusal to create a department in the first place.[34] It could be seen as analogous to removal of books from a library, and might be analyzed similarly, with courts forbidding unmistakable viewpoint discrimination while otherwise allowing universities to do as they wish. Even if that is the right approach, courts should and likely would give the authorities a great deal of room to maneuver; judges are hardly in a good position to order universities to maintain departments.

Admittedly, the line between case 16 and case 24 might seem thin. But removal of books, because of the viewpoint they endorse, gets close to the core of the free speech principle; it is in the same analytic category as book burning. By contrast, elimination of a department might depend, at least in part, on the allocation and expenditure of scarce resources. In general, it is not appropriate for courts to oversee decisions of that kind.

The line between case 17 and case 24 is thinner still. The two do seem very close. Ordering a university to buy books is not so different from ordering a university to maintain a department, though the latter is a more intrusive step than the former. We should be able to agree that courts should generally, and will generally, stay out of these domains.

25

Same as case 21 or case 24, but the relevant action comes from the state legislature. It is tempting to say that the analysis is the same, but if the action comes from the state legislature, issues of academic freedom are in play. Elimination of a comparative literature department, by a state legislature, would be puzzling, but it is hard to find viewpoint discrimination. Elimination of a gender studies department, by a state legislature, smacks of viewpoint discrimination. It might well be unconstitutional.

26

A state legislature forbids its public universities from teaching any course that "promotes identity politics," that "is based on theories that systemic racism, sexism, oppression, and privilege are inherent in the institutions of the United States," or that "refers to or endorses the idea of 'intersectionality.'"

The relevant law is almost certainly an unconstitutional form of viewpoint discrimination. It is not necessary to embrace broad ideas about academic freedom to suggest that if a legislature forbids faculty from teaching particular points of view, it must have a strong justification. A prohibition on teaching that the earth is flat would have such a justification; so, too, for a prohibition on teaching that the Holocaust did not happen. In both cases, the goal would be to prevent teachers from teaching demonstrable falsehoods. But if a legislature bans faculty from teaching courses that promote some political stance, and does so *because* it disapproves of that political stance, no such justification is available.

To be sure, we could put pressure on this conclusion. Suppose a state legislature forbids universities from teaching any course that "promotes Nazism" or "supports terrorism." Some people might be tempted to bite a large bullet and say that viewpoint discrimination is presumed to be invalid, period, and that intense opposition to a point of view does not justify a prohibition on teaching it, at least if it is not demonstrably false. That might seem to be an attractive approach, at least insofar as we are dealing with state or federal efforts to regulate what might be taught at universities. Under this view, a state legislature may not forbid universities from teaching courses that promote Nazism or support terrorism. That view does sound pretty extreme (though a prohibition on teaching any course that "supports terrorism" might be unacceptably vague).

An alternative and less extreme approach would insist that some points of view are so self-evidently harmful, and so self-evidently wrong, that officials may prohibit them from being taught as part of the university curriculum. The educational mission of the university might be invoked in support of such an approach. This alternative approach would seem consistent with the First Amendment, but we are in uncharted waters.

The principal advantage of the alternative approach is that it would cover apparently obvious cases, such as those involving Nazism or terrorism. The disadvantage is that it would produce serious line-drawing problems and a degree of contestation. One person's self-evident harm, and self-evident error, is another person's deep truth.

Even if we embrace the alternative and less extreme approach (and I think we should), the viewpoint-based bans described in the first paragraph above are very hard to defend. They also seem unacceptably vague and overbroad.

27

Same as case 26, but we are dealing with a state legislature's decision not to fund such courses, rather than a flat ban. The analysis is the same. Funding decisions are subject to the same First Amendment principles as bans.

28

Same as case 26, and similar to case 27, but the relevant decision comes from Congress or the president of the United States, acting through federal agencies. Same result. Federal funding decisions are subject to the same First Amendment principles as bans. It follows that federal funding decisions embodying viewpoint discrimination or content discrimination must be carefully scrutinized and will face a presumption of unconstitutionality. Even if the relevant actions are less sweeping and draconian than in case 26, they are likely to be invalidated.

29

A state legislature enacts a law stating that professors in public universities must "foster a culture of intellectual diversity." If they fail to do so, they might be fired. The background to the legislation shows unambiguously that it is an effort to ensure more airing of "conservative viewpoints."[35]

This is a troubling case, and it is not a straightforward one. On its face, the law is not viewpoint-based. It does not discriminate against any point of view. To be sure, it is content-based. One cannot know whether a professor is fostering intellectual diversity without knowing something about the content of the syllabus, and about what happens in the classroom. The background of the law makes it worse, though it is not fatal, because of the viewpoint neutrality of the law as written.

First Amendment law makes a distinction between "facial challenges"—which argue that a given piece of legislation is invalid "on its face"—and "as applied" challenges. A facial challenge could result in invalidation of a law in the abstract, before it is even applied. An as-applied challenge could result in invalidation of a law as applied to a particular institution or person. A law that explicitly requires "more attention to conservative points of view" would be subject to a facial challenge, and a strong one, because it is an effort to promote a particular viewpoint. But there is a reasonable argument that the law is not invalid on its face, because it could be applied in a way that is relatively innocuous and simply an effort to foster a (reasonable) range of (reasonable) opinions. Still, we could imagine convincing "as applied" challenges—as, for example, if a philosophy professor is punished for not sufficiently covering conservative views in a course on John Rawls (a liberal political philosopher).

In the abstract, the law is troubling from the constitutional point of view, but perhaps not unconstitutional. Still, it could easily be administered in a way that gives rise to a host of legitimate constitutional challenges.

30

Responding to an executive order from the president, the Department of Education issues a regulation denying federal funds to any university that does not "foster a culture of intellectual diversity" and make space for "a wide variety of viewpoints." The department establishes a working group, and a process, for assessing whether universities act in compliance with those requirements.

The analysis is the same as for case 29. In light of what seems to be the likely background, there is an argument that the regulation should be struck down on its face. But we could more readily imagine a successful "as applied" challenge.

31

A professor of philosophy makes sexually explicit videos with her husband. She considers them to be "instructional" and "fun." The videos are publicly available on the internet. The university asks her to take the videos down and to stop making them, and tells her that she will be disciplined and possibly fired if she refuses. She refuses.

This is not an easy case. On the one hand, the university may claim that its mission is compromised if members of its faculty are making sexually explicit videos, which could be (in its view) a "distraction at best" for students. Can a professor teach if students are aware that making such videos is the professor's hobby? On that view, the university is seeking to ensure that its educators can educate.

On the other hand, people generally have a First Amendment right to make such videos, and the university's view might prove too much: any expressive activity, including political activity, might distract students. Perhaps some students would be distracted and appalled if a professor endorses, or works for, certain politicians or causes. But acceptance of that argument would raise a serious risk of creating something analogous to a heckler's veto.[36] The question is whether the university can convincingly show that the educational mission is genuinely compromised. On the facts as stated, it probably cannot.

32

Same as case 31, except the professor is also the president of the university. This case is much easier for the university, which can plausibly argue that because of the distinctive role of the university's leader, various restrictions on speech-related activities are permissible even if they would be questionable or outright unacceptable for a professor without administrative responsibilities. This would be a plausible inference from *Pickering*.

33

A law professor writes a short book, attempting to explain what the First Amendment protects and does not protect on campus. Some of its conclusions are arguably wrong (as the professor himself is willing to acknowledge). Some of the professor's kind and generous colleagues write him detailed comments, to which he does not adequately respond. Some students, and some professors, are disappointed and even appalled by the book.

The university cannot punish the professor.[37]

· 4 ·

Public and Private

Let us now turn to a question that I have bracketed thus far: In the absence of a constitutional obligation, should private universities *choose* to follow the First Amendment? Recall that public universities are bound by the First Amendment and that private universities are not. As far as the Constitution is concerned, they can do what they want.

One size does not fit all. We can characterize universities in many different ways. A relevant distinction might be between universities that do not have any particular religious, sectarian, ethnic, political, or other identity, and those that define themselves by reference to such an identity. Boston University, Bowdoin College, Brown University, Vassar College, and Trinity College fall in the former category. Georgetown University, University of Notre Dame, Boston College, Brandeis University, and Brigham Young University fall in the latter category. Of course there is a continuum here, not a bright line. Georgetown, for example, is a Catholic university, but it is also a liberal arts university, dedicated to pluralism. Approximately half of its students are Catholic.[1] The same can be said of Boston College, where 70 percent of the students are Catholic.[2]

An all-purpose liberal arts university might be especially tempted to think that its educational mission calls for strict adherence to the First Amendment. It might well believe that First Amendment principles are the right ones, given that mission. Having assessed the consequences of following those principles, it might conclude, on reflection, that even if some of those consequences are jarring, most of them are good or even excellent. Importantly, it might also think that even if those principles are not perfect, they provide a ready-made foundation for a university's decisions, one that greatly simplifies its judgments and relieves it of the burden of building a foundation from scratch. For a private university, it might well be attractive to think and to say: *We will do what the Constitution says.*

But there are countervailing considerations. A liberal arts university might think that it is a particular kind of community, one that cannot and should not tolerate particular kinds of speech, simply because of the kind of community that it is. For example, it might think that it has a special duty to its students—say, to protect them against certain forms of humiliation, fear, or feelings of exclusion. It might want to forbid speech that members of its community might find horrifying or threatening, even if that speech would be protected by the First Amendment. It might even say that its educational mission calls for such restrictions.

Imagine, for example, that a university concludes that it is beyond the pale to say "Death to America!" or "Death to Jews!" or "Death to Israel!" or "Slavery was Great!" or "Women belong in the Bedroom!" As we have seen, all of these statements are likely protected by the First Amendment (unless they constitute a true threat or produce a clear and present danger). But a university might nevertheless want to prohibit this kind of speech on its campus, precisely because of the community that it seeks to be. Similarly, a university might ban the use of certain racial epithets, not only in face-to-face communications but more broadly, on the theory that use of such epithets is uniquely or distinctly associated with a system of racial caste. (Of course it might make some exceptions, as, for example, in readings of historical texts.) Or a university might say that a broader set of epithets will not be allowed in its community. I spare the reader a list of examples.

Alternatively, a liberal arts university might believe that members of its community should follow norms of patriotism. It might think that as a grateful part of the nation, it should inculcate values of respect for national traditions. For that reason, it might consider some speech to be beyond the pale even if that speech is protected by the First Amendment. If students or faculty say disloyal or harshly negative things about the United States of America, its traditions, and its values, such a university might be inclined to say: Some places, maybe, but not here.

To come to terms with these possibilities, we should acknowledge that more than one path would be defensible. It would be fully reasonable for a university to say that it will follow the First Amendment—period. Life might turn up problems that will make the university regret that choice or rethink it. But the basic idea has considerable appeal. I tend to think that for most universities, that is the best approach. See Appendix A for how it might look in practice.

Still, it might not be unreasonable for a university to make some exceptions, at least if they are surgical, clear, and specific. If a university says that norms of respect and inclusion call for some (narrowly and specifically defined) restrictions on what is commonly considered to be hate speech, there is no reason for outrage; disappointment and disagreement, perhaps, but not outrage. And if a university calls for principles of minimal civility (narrowly and specifically defined) with respect to national traditions, we might be able to respect that choice, too. (The danger, of course, is that mandatory patriotism might be inconsistent with the educational enterprise. Recall Justice Jackson's words: "Compulsory unification of opinion achieves only the unanimity of the graveyard." [3])

The analysis is different for institutions with a particular kind of identity. For example, a university with a distinctive religious mission might insist that a full-throated commitment to First Amendment principles is ill-suited to that mission. Such a university might well seek to inculcate or preserve certain values associated with its faith. Words that cast contempt on those values, or on that faith, might be forbidden. (For instance: "Catholicism is child abuse.") To the claim that such restrictions on speech curb freedom, such a university might say: "There are plenty of universities out there, and you are free to choose others. We exercise our own freedom by defining our community in a certain way." Fair enough.

We could imagine a variety of approaches here, from the most speech-protective to the more censorious.[4] Let me make a personal plea: *If a university is seeking to educate its students, it should minimize censorship, and clearly explain why it is allowing freedom for the speech that it hates.* That is broadly true, I suggest, even for institutions with a particular kind of identity and mission.

Then there are military academies: the United States Military Academy (West Point), the United States Naval Academy, the United States Air Force, the United States Coast Guard Academy, and the United States Merchant Marine Academy. These are, of course, public institutions, and so the First Amendment applies. But how? That is an exceedingly delicate and difficult question, one without clear answers from the Supreme Court. The military academies are preparing students for a career in military service, which has its own norms, including principles of hierarchy, discipline, and obedience. Insubordination of various kinds is not tolerated. In the United States Army, unlimited freedom of speech is not allowed, and it shouldn't be.[5] The United States Army need not allow a student organization called Students for the Ultimate Victory of Russia or Students for the Abolition of the United States Military. We could imagine far less obvious cases; suppose that the Naval Academy prohibits its faculty from writing things that are self-evidently inconsistent with the policies and goals of the United States. There could certainly be hard line-drawing problems here.

As of this writing, West Point prohibits "online unprofessional behavior" that "tends to discredit the military service, or presents a clear danger to loyalty, mission, or morale of other military or civilian personnel."[6] Furthermore, students may not "engag[e] in communication that is considered disrespectful toward superior officers," including "contemptuous or denunciatory language toward superior officers offline or through social media."[7] The Naval Academy has a student conduct code that includes: "You agree to be honorable in everything you do and say."[8]

Students at the Naval Academy are subject to multiple regulations that could affect what they might say. For example: "Midshipmen will conduct themselves with the utmost professionalism in all interpersonal interactions in all settings and at all times. Midshipmen will treat each and every person with dignity and respect."[9] In addition, midshipmen are directed to "[s]how deference to officers at all times by recognizing their presence and employing a courteous and respectful bearing and mode of speech toward them."[10] At official events or lectures, students should "[a]sk only questions appropriate to the rank of the speaker and the size of the audience."[11] If students are posting videos for online publication, they "must be in good taste and avoid offensive or inappropriate behavior that could bring discredit to the Navy or the USNA."[12]

Are these kinds of restrictions consistent with the First Amendment? It is clear that they would not be if they were imposed by, say, the University of Michigan, the University of Alabama, or the University of Oregon. There is also a serious question of whether the restrictions are unacceptably vague. Recall the requirement of fair notice.[13] Terms like "unprofessional behavior," "honorable," "courteous and respectful bearing and mode of speech," and "good taste" could easily be challenged as unduly vague, certainly as applied to borderline cases.[14] The overbreadth problem is also serious. Some of the restrictions would seem to forbid a lot of speech that the First Amendment protects.

At the same time, it is clear that military academies, as such, have a degree of flexibility to restrict speech simply because they are military academies, whose purpose is to train people to defend the nation. If West Point wants to ban its students from posting videos that are designed to undermine national security, or that celebrate the enemies of the United States of America, it is not running afoul of the United States Constitution. In my view, however, some of the current guidelines are too vague and too broad. They should be made more specific, and they should be narrowed.

Taking Sides

Should a university, as a university, take sides on public issues? Should it express a position on climate change? On civil rights? On immigration? On an ongoing war? On abortion rights?

To the general question, we could imagine a range of answers:

1. No, never
2. No, with one particular exception for self-preservation
3. No, with exceedingly narrow exceptions
4. Yes, if the issue is clear

Begin by isolating the relevant considerations. If a university takes a side on an issue, it might be able to increase the probability that the issue will be properly resolved (by its lights). Suppose the question is whether to support a constitutional right to an abortion. If, say, Yale University comes out in favor of a constitutional right to an abortion, perhaps it will be more likely that women will come to possess that right. But we should be careful not to overstate the point. If a university, as such, supports some outcome, it might do little or nothing to make that outcome more likely.

Typically, I think, that is the case. A statement by a university, if it occurs, is usually an expression of values, with little or no effect on the world. Still, we could imagine circumstances in which the university's position might matter.

On the other hand, any position, by any university, creates a host of problems. The first is *selectivity*. If a university condemns, say, an action by Israel, why won't it condemn an action by Russia? If a university condemns, say, an action by Russia, why doesn't it condemn actions by Cuba or Iran—or, for that matter, by the United States? These might be challenging questions to answer. No university is likely to want to create a Committee on Whom to Condemn.

If a university is thinking of condemning one action when a host of other candidates for condemnation lie on the horizon, its leaders might reasonably think: That way lies madness. So, too, if a university is asked to support or to deny the existence of a right. If a university embraces a right to choose abortion, what about the right to same-sex marriage? What about animal rights? What about the right to a well-paying job? What about the right to private property?

The second problem is *internal dispute*. The university might be asked to condemn the nation's failure to do enough about climate change. But many of its students and faculty might think that the nation should *not* do more about climate change. They might disagree on the merits. If the university where they study or work takes an official position opposed to theirs, they might feel both discredited and silenced. In a sense, the university would be purporting to speak in their name. As a result, they might be deterred from saying what they really think. If the university speaks, it might, in fact, undermine freedom of speech on the part of its members.

The third problem involves the university's *self-interest.* If the university takes a position on public matters, it will inevitably cause rancor. Some of the rancor will come from public officials. Some of it will come from donors. Some of it will come from students and alumni. A university might think that its own goals, and even its central mission, might be at risk if it wades into public debates. Why should it run that risk if it cherishes those goals and that mission? A clear and firm rule—*we do not take official positions*—would save the university a lot of trouble.

I have described this as the university's self-interest, but what we are speaking of here is not in any way petty or narrow. The university might think that its mission is an honorable one, of great value to society as a whole, and that any steps that threaten that mission bear a heavy burden of justification. That thought strongly argues against taking public positions or making public statements.

The University of Chicago's Kalven Committee, charged with examining "the University's role in political and social action," put it this way:

> The mission of the university is the discovery, improvement, and dissemination of knowledge. Its domain of inquiry and scrutiny includes all aspects and all values of society. A university faithful to its mission will provide enduring challenges to social values, policies, practices, and institutions.

By design and by effect, it is the institution which creates discontent with the existing social arrangements and proposes
new ones. In brief, a good university, like Socrates, will be
upsetting. The instrument of dissent and criticism is the individual faculty member or the individual student. The university is the home and sponsor of critics; it is not itself the
critic.[1]

It is an eloquent paragraph (see Appendix C for the full report),
but the last two sentences are too conclusory. They are not self-
justifying. Why isn't the university itself the critic? We should not
mistake a definition for an argument. But there is indeed an argument beneath the surface here: it is that if the university is to perform its social role, it cannot, realistically speaking, be "the critic."

To understand why, imagine that a university really is taking an
assortment of stands on the issues of the day. Perhaps it is in lock-
step with the central government. It agrees with it on everything,
or at least it says that it does. Perhaps it is associated with a political
movement on the left. Perhaps it is associated with a movement
on the right. It agrees with one or another movement on everything, or at least it says that it does. Or it agrees with a movement
on something of fundamental importance. In any of these cases,
the university will put a great deal of pressure on both its faculty
and its students. It might not insist that they agree. But if your institution clearly embraces particular positions, it will not be so easy
to reject them. If you work for a company that takes a strong stand
on, say, immigration issues, you might well hesitate before express-

ing disagreement. Something similar might be true for faculty. So too, some students might feel uncomfortable saying, for instance, that labor unions are not in the interest of working people, if their university is on record saying the opposite.

There is no formula here, but these considerations strongly suggest that for most universities, the right answer is either 1 ("no, never"), 2 ("no, with one particular exception for self-preservation"), or 3 ("no, with exceedingly narrow exceptions"). Because of its simplicity, answer 1 has considerable appeal. It is nearly right. But we can think of two types of cases in which the general rule might be overcome, leading us to answers 2 or 3.

The first is when the university is itself at risk. If, for example, political actors are acting in such a way as to endanger the future of the university, the university, as such, might be justified in speaking out. Such endangerment might occur if the government is depriving the university of essential funds. It might occur if the government is making it impossible or hard for the university to be the kind of community it seeks to be—as, for example, if the government is censoring certain kinds of speech, or conditioning funding on certain restrictions on speech. Self-protection can be seen as a legitimate reason—perhaps the only legitimate reason—for a university to speak in its own capacity.

There is an analogy within the federal government. As part of the executive branch, the Department of Justice is supposed to defend acts of Congress on constitutional grounds, even if it thinks that those acts are not, in fact, constitutional. But there is an exception for cases in which acts of Congress invade the prerogatives of the executive branch. In such cases, the Department of Justice is allowed to decline to defend such acts of Congress and thus to insist on its ability to engage in self-protection.[2] So too, perhaps, for universities, leading us to 2.

The second set of cases, which might lead us instead to 3, involve truly extraordinary circumstances—circumstances that, we might hope, will never occur in the United States. If there is an unmistakable threat of Nazism, or something close to it, sweeping the country, perhaps a university need not remain silent. Let us simply note that this category of cases is very small. It does not include serious issues of the day: immigration, climate change, criminal justice, the minimum wage, labor policy, public safety, public health.

The choice between 2 and 3 is not straightforward. We should favor 3 if it really can be cabined—if it does not lead to uncertainty and slippery slope problems. We should favor 2 if 3 is more trouble than it is worth. Reasonable people can differ, but I tend to support 2, by a whisker.

So we have our answer: *No, with one particular exception for self-preservation.*

· 6 ·

Let Freedom Ring

The set of principles implementing the commitment to free speech in the United States is a marvel—a triumph of the human spirit. Astonishingly, those principles are a product not of the founding generation or even of the Civil War period; they have been built since the 1950s.[1]

Protection of free speech is essential to democratic self-government. It is also essential to personal autonomy, learning, and self-development. Speech cannot be regulated or controlled on the grounds that people might be offended, hurt, upset, saddened, angered, outraged, scared, enraged, or humiliated. Free nations avoid the unanimity of the graveyard, or anything close to it.

It is important to distinguish among viewpoint-based, content-based, and content-neutral restrictions. If we link freedom of speech and democratic goals, the distinction among those three kinds of restrictions makes a great deal of sense. Restrictions on speech should be forbidden in cases in which public officials are least likely to be trustworthy, and most likely to be compromising or "skewing" the system of democratic deliberation. It is for that reason that viewpoint-based restrictions are presumed to be invalid.

It is true, of course, that autonomy can be compromised by content-neutral restrictions. If you are told that you cannot sing loudly on the street after midnight, you might feel that your autonomy has been reduced. But when restrictions are content-neutral, government might well have sufficiently strong justifications for imposing them. Note, too, that sufficiently strong justifications are required.[2] If a nation respects free speech, it does not give anything like a green light to all content-neutral restrictions. Peace and quiet are important, but tyrants like peace and quiet too much. Societies need a little noise.

The commitment of free speech is general, and general propositions do not decide concrete questions. With respect to speech, no one can be an absolutist. No reasonable person believes that the right to free speech protects perjury and bribery. No reasonable person believes that the right to free speech protects conspiracies to fix prices, or forbids government from punishing people from lying to the authorities on their job applications.

The educational setting is distinctive. Because of their missions, colleges and universities can regulate speech in various ways. In a class on Shakespeare, teachers and students can be directed to focus on Shakespeare, not on climate change or immigration. No one has a right to shout down speakers. No one has a right to take over buildings. There is no constitutional right to plagiarize. Professors and administrators have particular roles, and because of those roles, universities can impose certain constraints on what they may say. Even so, let us be clear: Universities, and those who oversee or regulate them, should respect the set of principles implementing the commitment to free speech.

Norms of civility, mutual respect, and considerateness are exceedingly important, and they should be cultivated and inculcated. But they are norms, not laws. Students and faculty should not be punished for incivility or offensiveness. Whether public or private, universities should permit members of their communities to say things that are disturbing, jarring, horrifying, enraging, scary, or disruptive. The best response to errors, and to offensive or horrifying speech, is more speech, not punishment. Universities exist to promote learning. They are an arsenal of democracy.

Let freedom ring—on public streets, in public parks, and on campus.

A Proposed Framework

Here is a very short framework that colleges and universities might consider as they adopt or rethink their own approaches to free speech on campus. One size does not fit all, as they say, but perhaps one size fits almost all.

1. The University is firmly committed to freedom of speech. That commitment entails a belief in the importance of dialogue, disagreement, diversity, and pluralism. The University welcomes multiple points of view. It aims to promote independent thinking and the fearless pursuit of truth. Speech should never be restricted or punished because some people find it illogical, distasteful, hurtful, offensive, upsetting, wrongheaded, foolish, irreverent, or nonsensical. To promote learning, the University seeks to promote safe spaces for a wide range of ideas.

2. If speech is not protected by the First Amendment and is inconsistent with criminal or civil law, the University need not tolerate it. Criminal conspiracy, criminal solicitation, commercial fraud, and bribery are not welcome here. The same is true of libel, direct threats, and sexual harassment, as defined by law.

If speech is directed to incite and likely to incite imminent lawless action, it will not be permitted.

3. The commitment to freedom of speech does not mean that members of the university community may (a) disrupt or prevent the speech of others, (b) block access to or take over buildings, (c) disrupt classes, (d) shut down or unreasonably interfere with campus activities, (e) violate legitimate time, place, and manner restrictions, or (f) trespass on private property. Absent special circumstances, protest activities that do not fall in the foregoing categories are presumed to be acceptable.

4. The commitment to freedom of speech does not protect plagiarism and other misrepresentations of the authorship of a work. Nothing in the commitment to freedom of speech forbids restrictions on the use of artificial intelligence, designed to ensure that the work of students and faculty is their own.

5. The educational mission of the University may entail specific, narrowly drawn restrictions on speech, designed to ensure that teachers teach and that students learn. For example, both teachers and students may be asked to focus classroom time on the subject of their courses, and students may be asked to focus their assignments and examinations on that subject. Any such restrictions must respect the principles laid out in (1) above.

The Chicago Principles

Report of the Committee on Freedom of Expression

The Committee on Freedom of Expression at the University of Chicago was appointed in July 2014 by President Robert J. Zimmer and Provost Eric D. Isaacs "in light of recent events nationwide that have tested institutional commitments to free and open discourse." The Committee's charge was to draft a statement "articulating the University's overarching commitment to free, robust, and uninhibited debate and deliberation among all members of the University's community."

The Committee has carefully reviewed the University's history, examined events at other institutions, and consulted a broad range of individuals both inside and outside the University. This statement reflects the long-standing and distinctive values of the University of Chicago and affirms the importance of maintaining and, indeed, celebrating those values for the future.

From its very founding, the University of Chicago has dedicated itself to the preservation and celebration of the freedom of expression as an essential element of the University's culture. In 1902, in his address marking the University's decennial, President William Rainey Harper declared that "the principle of complete freedom of speech on all subjects has from the beginning been regarded as fundamental in the University of Chicago" and that "this principle can neither now nor at any future time be called in question."

Thirty years later, a student organization invited William Z. Foster, the Communist Party's candidate for President, to lecture on campus. This triggered a storm of protest from critics both on and off campus. To those who condemned the University for allowing the event, President Robert M. Hutchins responded that "our students . . . should have freedom to discuss any problem that presents itself." He insisted that the "cure" for ideas we oppose "lies through open discussion rather than through inhibition."

On a later occasion, Hutchins added that "free inquiry is indispensable to the good life, that universities exist for the sake of such inquiry, [and] that without it they cease to be universities." In 1968, at another time of great turmoil in universities, President Edward H. Levi, in his inaugural address, celebrated "those virtues which from the beginning and until now have characterized our institution." Central to the values of the University of Chicago, Levi explained, is a profound commitment to "freedom of inquiry." This freedom, he proclaimed, "is our inheritance."

More recently, President Hanna Holborn Gray observed that "education should not be intended to make people comfortable, it is meant to make them think. Universities should be expected to provide the conditions within which hard thought, and therefore strong disagreement, independent judgment, and the questioning of stubborn assumptions, can flourish in an environment of the greatest freedom."

The words of Harper, Hutchins, Levi, and Gray capture both the spirit and the promise of the University of Chicago. Because the University is committed to free and open inquiry in all matters, it guarantees all members of the University community the broadest possible latitude to speak, write, listen, challenge, and learn. Except insofar as limitations on that freedom are necessary to the functioning of the University, the University of Chicago fully respects and supports the freedom of all members of the University community "to discuss any problem that presents itself." Of course, the ideas of different members of the University community will often and quite naturally conflict. But it is not the proper role of the University to attempt to shield individuals from ideas and opinions they find unwelcome, disagreeable, or even deeply offensive.

Although the University greatly values civility, and although all members of the University community share in the responsibility for maintaining a climate of mutual respect, concerns about civility and mutual respect can never be used as a justification for closing off discussion of ideas, however offensive or disagreeable those ideas may be to some members of our community. The freedom to debate and discuss the merits of competing ideas does not, of course, mean that individuals may say whatever they wish, wherever they wish. The University may restrict expression that violates the law, that falsely defames a specific individual, that constitutes a genuine threat or harassment, that unjustifiably invades substantial privacy or confidentiality interests, or that is otherwise directly incompatible with the functioning of the University. In addition, the University may reasonably regulate the time, place, and manner of expression to ensure that it does not disrupt the ordinary activities of the University.

But these are narrow exceptions to the general principle of freedom of expression, and it is vitally important that these exceptions never be used in a manner that is inconsistent with the University's commitment to a completely free and open discussion of ideas. In a word, the University's fundamental commitment is to the principle that debate or deliberation may not be suppressed because the ideas put forth are thought by some or even by most members of the University community to be offensive, unwise, immoral, or wrong-headed. It is for the individual members of the University community, not for the University as an institution, to make those judgments for themselves, and to act on those judgments not by seeking to suppress speech, but by openly and vigorously contesting the ideas that they oppose. Indeed, fostering the ability of members of the University community to engage in such debate and deliberation in an effective and responsible manner is an essential part of the University's educational mission.

As a corollary to the University's commitment to protect and promote free expression, members of the University community must also act in conformity with the principle of free expression. Although members of the University community are free to criticize and contest the views expressed on campus, and to criticize and contest speakers who are invited to express their views on campus, they may not obstruct or otherwise interfere with the freedom of others to express views they reject or even loathe. To this end, the University has a solemn responsibility not only to promote a lively and fearless freedom of debate and deliberation, but also to protect that freedom when others attempt to restrict it.

As Robert M. Hutchins observed, without a vibrant commitment to free and open inquiry, a university ceases to be a university. The University of Chicago's long-standing commitment to this principle lies at the very core of our University's greatness. That is our inheritance, and it is our promise to the future.

GEOFFREY R. STONE, Edward H. Levi Distinguished Service Professor of Law, *Chair*

MARIANNE BERTRAND, Chris P. Dialynas Distinguished Service Professor of Economics, Booth School of Business

ANGELA OLINTO, Homer J. Livingston Professor, Department of Astronomy and Astrophysics, Enrico Fermi Institute, and the College

MARK SIEGLER, Lindy Bergman Distinguished Service Professor of Medicine and Surgery

DAVID A. STRAUSS, Gerald Ratner Distinguished Service Professor of Law

KENNETH W. WARREN, Fairfax M. Cone Distinguished Service Professor, Department of English and the College

AMANDA WOODWARD, William S. Gray Professor, Department of Psychology and the College

Committee on Freedom of Expression at the University of Chicago, Report of the Committee on Freedom of Expression (*Chicago: University of Chicago, 2014*), https://provost.uchicago.edu/reports.

The Kalven Report

Kalven Committee: Report on the University's Role in Political and Social Action

Report of a faculty committee, under the chairmanship of Harry Kalven, Jr. Committee appointed by President George W. Beadle. Report published in the Record, Vol. I, No. 1, November 11, 1967.

The Committee was appointed in February 1967 by President George W. Beadle and requested to prepare "a statement on the University's role in political and social action." The Committee conceives its function as principally that of providing a point of departure for discussion in the University community of this important question.

The Committee has reviewed the experience of the University in such matters as its participation in neighborhood redevelopment, its defense of academic freedom in the Broyles Bill inquiry of the 1940s and again in the Jenner Committee hearings of the early 1950s, its opposition to the Disclaimer Affidavit in the National Defense Education Act of 1958, its reappraisal of the criteria by which it rents the off-campus housing it owns, and its position on furnishing the rank of male students to Selective Service. In its own discussions, the Committee has found a deep consensus on the appropriate role of the university in political and social action. It senses some popular misconceptions about that role and wishes, therefore, simply to reaffirm a few old truths and a cherished tradition.

A university has a great and unique role to play in fostering the development of social and political values in a society. The role is defined by the distinctive mission of the university and defined too by the distinctive characteristics of the university as a community. It is a role for the long term. The mission of the university is the discovery, improvement, and dissemination of knowledge. Its domain of inquiry and scrutiny includes all aspects and all values of society. A university faithful to its mission will provide enduring challenges to social values, policies, practices, and institutions. By design and by effect, it is the institution which creates discontent with the existing social arrangements and proposes new ones. In brief, a good university, like Socrates, will be upsetting. The instrument of dissent and criticism is the individual faculty member or the individual student. The university is the home and sponsor of critics; it is not itself the critic.

It is, to go back once again to the classic phrase, a community of scholars. To perform its mission in the society, a university must sustain an extraordinary environment of freedom of inquiry and maintain an independence from political fashions, passions, and pressures. A university, if it is to be true to its faith in intellectual inquiry, must embrace, be hospitable to, and encourage the widest diversity of views within its own community. It is a community but only for the limited, albeit great, purposes of teaching and research. It is not a club, it is not a trade association, it is not a lobby. Since the university is a community only for these limited and distinctive purposes, it is a community which cannot take collective action on the issues of the day without endangering the conditions for its existence and effectiveness.

There is no mechanism by which it can reach a collective position without inhibiting that full freedom of dissent on which it thrives. It cannot insist that all of its members favor a given view of social policy; if it takes collective action, therefore, it does so at the price of censuring any minority who do not agree with the view adopted. In brief, it is a community which cannot resort to majority vote to reach positions on public issues. The neutrality of the university as an institution arises then not from a lack of courage nor out of indifference and insensitivity. It arises out of respect for free inquiry and the obligation to cherish a diversity of viewpoints. And this neutrality as an institution has its complement in the fullest freedom for its faculty and students as individuals to participate in political action and social protest. It finds its complement, too, in the obligation of the university to provide a forum for the most searching and candid discussion of public issues.

Moreover, the sources of power of a great university should not be misconceived. Its prestige and influence are based on integrity and intellectual competence; they are not based on the circumstance that it may be wealthy, may have political contacts, and may have influential friends. From time to time instances will arise in which the society, or segments of it, threaten the very mission of the university and its values of free inquiry. In such a crisis, it becomes the obligation of the university as an institution to oppose such measures and actively to defend its interests and its values. There is another context in which questions as to the appropriate role of the university may possibly arise, situations involving university ownership of property, its receipt of funds, its awarding of honors, its membership in other organizations. Here, of necessity, the university, however it acts, must act as an institution in its corporate capacity. In the exceptional instance, these corporate activities of the university may appear so incompatible with paramount social values as to require careful assessment of the consequences.

These extraordinary instances apart, there emerges, as we see it, a heavy presumption against the university taking collective action or expressing opinions on the political and social issues of the day, or modifying its corporate activities to foster social or political values, however compelling and appealing they may be. These are admittedly matters of large principle, and the application of principle to an individual case will not be easy. It must always be appropriate, therefore, for faculty or students or administration to question, through existing channels such as the Committee of the Council or the Council, whether in light of these principles the University in particular circumstances is playing its proper role. Our basic conviction is that a great university can perform greatly for the betterment of society. It should not, therefore, permit itself to be diverted from its mission into playing the role of a second-rate political force or influence.

HARRY KALVEN, Jr., *Chairman*

JOHN HOPE FRANKLIN

GWIN J. KOLB

GEORGE STIGLER

JACOB GETZELS

JULIAN GOLDSMITH

GILBERT F. WHITE

Special Comment by Mr. Stigler:

I agree with the report as drafted, except for the statements in the fifth paragraph from the end as to the role of the university when it is acting in its corporate capacity. As to this matter, I would prefer the statement in the following form:

> The university when it acts in its corporate capacity as employer and property owner should, of course, conduct its affairs with honor. The university should not use these corporate activities to foster any moral or political values because such use of its facilities will impair its integrity as the home of intellectual freedom.

Kalven Committee, Report on the University's Role in Political and Social Action (Chicago: University of Chicago, 1967), https://provost.uchicago.edu/reports/report-universitys-role-political-and-social-action.

Notes

Preface

1. W. Va. State Bd. of Educ. v. Barnette, 319 U.S. 624, 641 (1943).

Introduction

1. U.S. Const. amend. I.

2. U.S. Const. amend. XIV.

3. Gitlow v. New York, 268 U.S. 652 (1925).

4. For an overview, see Cass R. Sunstein, *How to Interpret the Constitution* (Princeton, NJ: Princeton University Press, 2023).

5. We could find or imagine critiques from many different directions. For example, Catharine A. MacKinnon, "Weaponizing the First Amendment: An Equality Reading," *Virginia Law Review* 106, no. 6 (2020): 1223–1283, would suggest a quite different approach from that suggested by current law, though we could imagine courts moving in her direction, especially in the educational context.

6. Note, however, that states may attempt to require universities to follow the First Amendment. In 1992, California enacted the Leonard Law, which "applies First Amendment requirements to the disciplinary regulations of California's private universities." Elena Kagan, "When a Speech Code is a Speech Code: The Stanford Policy and the Theory of Incidental Restraints," *UC Davis Law Review* 29, no. 3 (Spring 1996): 958n2. Under this

law, obligations imposed on non-religious private universities are identical to those imposed on public universities. Interestingly, it might be urged that laws that require private universities to follow the First Amendment turn out to violate . . . the First Amendment! That argument is not crazy, but I will not engage it here.

7. Abrams v. United States, 250 U.S. 616, 630 (Holmes, J., dissenting).

8. For an argument that they should do so, see Erwin Chemerinsky and Howard Gillman, *Free Speech on Campus* (New Haven, CT: Yale University Press, 2017). I will explore that issue in Chapter 4.

1. Some General Points

1. See, generally, Edna Ullmann-Margalit, *The Emergence of Norms* (Oxford: Clarendon Press, 1978).

2. See, generally, Edna Ullmann-Margalit, *Normal Rationality: Decisions and Social Order,* ed. Avishai Margalit and Cass R. Sunstein (Oxford: Oxford University Press, 2017).

3. See Cass R. Sunstein, *Conformity: The Power of Social Influences* (New York: New York University Press, 2019).

4. Brandenburg v. Ohio, 395 U.S. 444, 447 (1969) (per curiam).

5. Douglas Laycock, "The Clear and Present Danger Test," *Journal of Supreme Court History* 25, no. 2 (2000): 161–186.

6. See, e.g., Hess v. Indiana, 414 U.S. 105, 109 (1973).

7. False commercial advertising, see Cent. Hudson Gas & Elec. Corp. v. Pub. Serv. Comm'n of N.Y., 447 U.S. 557, 563 (1980) ("[T]here can be no constitutional objection to the suppression of commercial messages that do not accurately inform the public about lawful activity."). Obscenity, see Miller v. California, 413 U.S. 15 (1973). Defamation and libel, see N.Y. Times Co. v. Sullivan, 376 U.S. 254 (1964). "True threats," see Counterman v. Colorado, 600 U.S. 66, 72 (2023); Watts v. United States, 394 U.S. 705, 708 (1969). Sexual harassment, see J. M. Balkin, "Free Speech and Hostile Environments," *Co-*

lumbia Law Review 99, no. 8 (Dec. 1999): 2295–2320; Eugene Volokh, "Freedom of Speech and Workplace Harassment," *UCLA Law Review* 39, no. 6 (Aug. 1992): 1791–1872; Eugene Volokh, "What Speech Does 'Hostile Work Environment' Harassment Law Restrict?" *Georgetown Law Journal* 85, no. 3 (February 1997): 627–648, 647. Criminal solicitation, see Giboney v. Empire Storage & Ice Co., 336 U.S. 490, 502 (1949) ("[I]t has never been deemed an abridgement of freedom of speech or press to make a course of conduct illegal merely because the conduct was in part initiated, evidenced, or carried out by means of language, either spoken, written, or printed."). Perjury, see United States v. Dunnigan, 507 U.S. 87, 97 (1993) ("To uphold the integrity of our trial system, we have said that the constitutionality of perjury statutes is unquestioned."). Fraud, see, e.g., Donaldson v. Read Magazine, Inc., 333 U.S. 178 (1948).

8. The statement in text assumes a suitable definition. On the status of lies and falsehoods, see Cass R. Sunstein, "Falsehoods and the First Amendment," *Harvard Journal of Law & Technology* 33, no. 2 (Spring 2020): 388–426.

9. A classic discussion is Paul Goldstein, "Copyright and the First Amendment," *Columbia Law Review* 70, no. 6 (June 1970): 983–1057.

10. This is so even though many imaginable restrictions on the use of ChatGPT and other large language models would raise serious constitutional questions. See Cass R. Sunstein, "Artificial Intelligence and the First Amendment," *George Washington Law Review* 92 (forthcoming) (on file at SSRN).

11. Even so, they may not discriminate on the basis of viewpoint, which means that they cannot carve out one category of unprotected speech, defined in terms of viewpoint, for regulation or punishment. R.A.V. v. City of St. Paul, 505 U.S. 377 (1992); Rosenberger v. Rector & Visitors of the Univ. of Va., 515 U.S. 819, 829 (1995).

12. See Geoffrey R. Stone, "Content Regulation and the First Amendment," *William & Mary Law Review* 25, no. 2 (Winter 1983): 189–252.

13. *R.A.V.*, 505 U.S. at 388; *Rosenberger*, 515 U.S. at 829. See in particular this illuminating passage from *Rosenberger*:

When the government targets not subject matter, but particular views taken by speakers on a subject, the violation of the First Amendment is all the more blatant. Viewpoint discrimination is thus an egregious form of content discrimination. The government must abstain from regulating speech when the specific motivating ideology or the opinion or perspective of the speaker is the rationale for the restriction.

14. It might be possible to argue that the prohibition on price-fixing is not viewpoint-based, on the theory is that the prohibition is designed not to prevent speech, but a kind of act. I acknowledge this point without embracing it here. It is tempting, and too easy, to characterize words that one wishes to ban as "acts."

15. See Reed v. Town of Gilbert, 576 U.S. 155, 165 (2015) ("[S]trict scrutiny applies either when a law is content based on its face or when the purpose and justification for the law are content based.").

16. See, e.g., Clark v. Cmty. for Creative Non-Violence, 468 U.S. 288, 293 (1984) ("[R]estrictions of this kind are valid provided that they are justified without reference to the content of the regulated speech, that they are narrowly tailored to serve a significant governmental interest, and that they leave open ample alternative channels for communication of the information."); see generally Geoffrey R. Stone, "Content-Neutral Restrictions," *University of Chicago Law Review* 54, no. 1 (1987): 46–118. There is also a distinction between public forums and nonpublic or limited public forums; the latter may be subject to broader regulation. See *Rosenberger,* 515 U.S. at 829. I am largely bracketing that issue here, though we could produce scenarios that would test it.

17. See Grayned v. City of Rockford, 408 U.S. 104, 112 (1972) (noting with approval that the ordinance gave "'fair notice to those to whom [it] [was] directed'").

18. See Soglin v. Kauffman, 418 F.2d 163 (7th Cir. 1969) (finding that a "misconduct" standard was insufficiently specific).

19. This statement cannot be found in any Supreme Court opinion, and hence it cannot be said to be a necessary reading of current law. Compare,

e.g., B.H. ex rel. Hawk v. Easton Area Sch. Dist., 725 F.3d 293, 316 (3d Cir. 2013) ("[S]weeping and total deference to school officials is incompatible with the Supreme Court's teachings"), with LaVine v. Blaine Sch. Dist., 257 F.3d 981, 988 (9th Cir. 2001) ("[A] school need not tolerate student speech that is inconsistent with its basic educational mission."). Nevertheless, no other formulation can account for established understandings, and the formulation fits well with *Pickering* and *Connick*, discussed below.

20. It would be possible to argue that the phrase "essential to" is too strong and that it should be replaced by "central to" or "a legitimate part of." For useful discussion, see Robert Post, "The Classic First Amendment Tradition Under Stress: Freedom of Speech and the University," in *The Free Speech Century*, ed. Lee C. Bollinger and Geoffrey R. Stone (New York: Oxford University Press, 2018); Robert Post, "Academic Freedom and the Constitution," in *Who's Afraid of Academic Freedom?*, ed. Akeel Bilgrami and Jonathan R. Cole (New York: Columbia University Press, 2015); Robert Post, "Comment on Freedom of Expression in American Legal Education," *Hofstra Law Review* 51, no. 3 (Spring 2023): 667–678. Compare to Morse v. Frederick, 551 U.S. 393, 423 (2007) (Alito, J., concurring) (objecting to a test centered on a school's "educational mission" on the grounds that "[t]he 'educational mission' of the public schools is defined by the elected and appointed public officials with authority over the schools and by the school administrators and faculty," such that as a result, "some public schools have defined their educational missions as including the inculcation of whatever political and social views are held by the members of these groups").

21. Post, "Classic First Amendment Tradition."

22. Pickering v. Bd. of Educ., 391 U.S. 563 (1968).

23. *Pickering*, 391 U.S. at 570.

24. *Pickering*, 391 U.S. at 572–573.

25. *Pickering*, 391 U.S. at 573.

26. Connick v. Myers, 461 U.S. 138 (1983).

27. Post, "Classic First Amendment Tradition," 108.

28. Post, "Classic First Amendment Tradition," 108.

29. Post, "Classic First Amendment Tradition," 112.

30. Post, "Classic First Amendment Tradition," 113.

31. Post, "Classic First Amendment Tradition," 114.

32. Post, "Classic First Amendment Tradition," 110.

33. See Urofsky v. Gilmore, 216 F.3d 401 (2000), which says: "Appellees' insistence that the Act violates their rights of academic freedom amounts to a claim that the academic freedom of professors is not only a professional norm, but also a constitutional right. We disagree. It is true, of course, that homage has been paid to the ideal of academic freedom in a number of Supreme Court opinions, often with reference to the First Amendment . . . Despite these accolades, the Supreme Court has never set aside a state regulation on the basis that it infringed a First Amendment right to academic freedom." *Urofsky*, 216 F.3d at 411–412. For general discussion, see Keith E. Whittington, "Professorial Speech, the First Amendment, and Legislative Restrictions on Classroom Discussions," *Wake Forest Law Review* 58, no. 2 (2023): 463–524.

34. Or so an intolerably young law professor once argued. See Cass R. Sunstein, *Democracy and the Problem of Free Speech* (New York: The Free Press, 1993).

35. See Mahanoy Area Sch. Dist. v. B.L. *ex rel.* Levy, 141 S. Ct. 2038 (2021); *Morse*, 551 U.S. at 393; Hazelwood Sch. Dist. v. Kuhlmeier, 484 U.S. 260 (1988); Bethel Sch. Dist. No. 403 v. Fraser, 478 U.S. 675 (1986); Tinker v. Des Moines Indep. Cmty. Sch. Dist., 393 U.S. 503 (1969). In *Mahanoy*, the Court said this:

> This Court has previously outlined three specific categories of student speech that schools may regulate in certain circumstances: (1) "indecent," "lewd," or "vulgar" speech uttered during a school assembly on school grounds; (2) speech, uttered during a class trip, that promotes "illegal drug use"; and (3) speech that others may reasonably perceive as "bear[ing] the imprimatur of the school," such as that appearing in a school-sponsored newspaper. Finally, in *Tinker*, we said schools have a special interest in regulating speech that "materially disrupts classwork or involves substantial

> disorder or invasion of the rights of others." These special characteristics
> call for special leeway when schools regulate speech that occurs under its
> supervision.

Mahanoy, 141 S. Ct. at 2045 (citations omitted). These statements were made in course of discussions of "schools," where the Court has been alert to the fact that the relevant students are typically minors and educators are acting *in loco parentis*. In colleges and universities, by contrast, the relevant students are typically adults. See *Mahanoy*, 141 S. Ct. at 2049 n.2 (Alito, J., concurring) ("[F]or several reasons, including the age, independence, and living arrangements of [college] students, regulation of their speech may raise very different questions from those presented" in the primary and secondary school context).

36. *Mahanoy*, 141 S. Ct. at 2046.

37. See generally *Fraser*, 478 U.S. at 675.

38. The Supreme Court has, of course, spoken on relevant issues, and I shall draw on the decided cases at multiple points. See, e.g., Papish v. Bd. of Curators of the Univ. of Mo., 410 U.S. 667 (1973); Rosenberger v. Rector & Visitors of the Univ. of Va., 515 U.S. 819 (1995); Healy v. James, 408 U.S. 169 (1972). Compare with Norton v. Discipline Comm. of E. Tenn. State Univ., 399 U.S. 906, 907 (1970) (Marshall, J., dissenting from denial of certiorari) (criticizing the Court's decision to decline review of expulsion of students from state university arising from leafletting activity).

39. *Healy*, 408 U.S. at 180.

40. See Cohen v. California, 403 U.S. 15 (1971).

2. Students

1. Rosenberger v. Rector & Visitors of the Univ. of Va., 515 U.S. 819, 829 (1995) ("The government must abstain from regulating speech when the specific motivating ideology or the opinion or perspective of the speaker is the rationale for the restriction").

2. *Rosenberger,* 515 U.S. at 829.

3. Ward v. Rock Against Racism, 491 U.S. 781 (1989) (concluding that content-neutral municipal noise regulation satisfied First Amendment scrutiny).

4. Brandenburg v. Ohio, 395 U.S. 444, 447 (1969) (per curiam); Douglas Laycock, "The Clear and Present Danger Test," *Journal of Supreme Court History* 25, no. 2 (2000): 161–186.

5. *Merriam-Webster,* s.v. "intifada," accessed Dec. 19, 2023, https://www.merriam-webster.com/dictionary/intifada.

6. *Merriam-Webster,* "intifada." We could imagine a variation on this case that would put pressure on the basic conclusion. Suppose, for example, that a university reasonably believes that the inevitable consequence of the march would be a violent confrontation among students. Must the university deploy a security force? At what expense?

7. Collin v. Smith, 578 F.2d 1197 (7th Cir. 1978) (allowing a Nazi march in Skokie, Illinois).

8. *Brandenburg,* 395 U.S. at 447.

9. Brown v. Bd. of Regents of Univ. of Nebraska, 640 F. Supp. 674, 681 (D. Neb. 1986) (holding that university's decision to cancel showing of controversial film on the basis of its "ideological viewpoint" violated the First Amendment).

10. *Brandenburg,* 395 U.S. at 447.

11. City of Austin, Texas v. Reagan Nat'l Advert. of Austin, LLC, 596 U.S. 61, 69 (2022) (explaining that if a regulation applies to particular speech "because of the topic discussed or the idea or message expressed," it is subject to strict scrutiny) (quoting Reed v. Town of Gilbert, 576 U.S. 155, 163 (2015)).

12. *Brandenburg* 395 U.S. at 447.

13. See Counterman v. Colorado, 600 U.S. 66, 72 (2023). The Court's first full paragraph tells the tale:

> True threats of violence are outside the bounds of First Amendment protection and punishable as crimes. Today we consider a criminal conviction

for communications falling within that historically unprotected category. The question presented is whether the First Amendment still requires proof that the defendant had some subjective understanding of the threatening nature of his statements. We hold that it does, but that a mental state of recklessness is sufficient. The State must show that the defendant consciously disregarded a substantial risk that his communications would be viewed as threatening violence. The State need not prove any more demanding form of subjective intent to threaten another.

Counterman, 600 U.S. at 69.

14. *Counterman,* 600 U.S. at 74.

15. Compare this to the discussion of Beauharnais v. Illinois, 343 U.S. 250 (1952) in case 13.

16. *Counterman* 600 U.S. at 69.

17. Chaplinsky v. New Hampshire, 315 U.S. 568 (1942), is the source of the "fighting words" doctrine. There the Court said that the Constitution does not protect "the lewd and obscene, the profane, the libelous, and the insulting or 'fighting' words—those which, by their very utterance, inflict injury or tend to incite an immediate breach of the peace." *Chaplinsky,* 315 U.S. at 572. The Court quoted a previous decision: "Resort to epithets or personal abuse is not in any proper sense communication of information or opinion safeguarded by the Constitution, and its punishment as a criminal act would raise no question under that instrument." *Chaplinsky,* 315 U.S. at 572 (quoting Cantwell v. Connecticut, 310 U.S. 296, 309–310 (1940)). It is not clear how much of this remains good law. The lewd, the obscene, and the libelous are sometimes protected by the First Amendment as it now stands. On fighting words, see Collin v. Smith, 578 F.2d 1197 (7th Cir. 1978): "The Court in Chaplinsky affirmed a conviction under a statute that, as authoritatively construed, applied only to words with a direct tendency to cause violence by the persons to whom, individually, the words were addressed. A conviction for less than words that at least tend to incite an immediate breach of the peace cannot be justified under Chaplinsky."

18. See, e.g., People v. Marquan M., 19 N.E.3d 480 (N.Y. 2014). As then-Judge Alito noted in Saxe v. State Coll. Area Sch. Dist., 240 F.3d 200, 204 (3rd Cir. 2001), "[t]here is no categorical 'harassment exception' to the First Amendment's free speech clause." Regarding cyberbullying, the law is in a state of development; see Doe v. Hopkinton Public Schools, 19 F.4d 493 (1st Cir. 2021); Norris v. Cape Elizabeth, 969 F.3d 12 (1st Cir. 2020); S.J.W. ex rel. Wilson v. Lee's Summit R-7 Sch. Dist., 696 F.3d 771, 778 (8th Cir. 2012); see generally Kirsten Hallmark, "Death by Words: Do United States Statutes Hold Cyberbullies Liable for Their Victims' Suicide?," Houston Law Review 60, no. 3 (Winter 2023): 727–756.

19. Matal v. Tam, 582 U.S. 218, 220, 137 S. Ct. 1744, 1749 (2017) ("Giving offense is a viewpoint . . . '[T]he public expression of ideas may not be prohibited merely because the ideas are themselves offensive to some of their hearers.'") (quoting Street v. New York, 394 U.S. 576, 592 (1969)).

20. For a comparison, see Collin, 578 F.2d 1197.

21. Beauharnais, 343 U.S. 250. This statute is quoted in Beauharnais, 343 U.S. at 251.

22. Beauharnais, 343 U.S. at 258.

23. New York Times v. Sullivan, 376 U.S. 254 (1964).

24. R.A.V. v. City of St. Paul, 505 U.S. 377 (1992).

25. See Cass R. Sunstein, "Artificial Intelligence and the First Amendment," George Washington Law Review 92 (forthcoming 2024) (on file at SSRN), available at https://papers.ssrn.com/sol3/papers.cfm?abstract_id =4431251.

26. Grayned v. City of Rockford, 408 U.S. 104 (1972) (emphasizing the importance of notice); Soglin v. Kauffman, 418 F.2d 163 (7th Cir. 1969) (the term "misconduct" as the standard for behavior is not clear enough to provide students with notice about what is allowed and what is forbidden).

27. Reno v. Am. C.L. Union, 521 U.S. 844, 880 (1997) (rejecting speech regulation that conveys the "powers of censorship, in the form of a 'heckler's veto,' upon any opponent of indecent speech"); Hill v. Colorado, 530 U.S. 703,

734 n.43 (2000) (regulations are "problematic" if they allow "single, private actor to unilaterally silence a speaker even as to willing listeners").

28. Schenck v. Pro-Choice Network of W.N.Y., 519 U.S. 357 (1997) (upholding buffer zones around abortion clinics); *Hill,* 530 U.S. at 729–730 (similar).

29. *Brandenburg* 395 U.S. at 447.

30. Clark v. Cmty. for Creative Non-Violence, 468 U.S. 288, 293 (1984).

31. This is a variation on the events described in Jaweed Kaleem, "'Please leave!' A Jewish UC Berkeley dean confronts pro-Palestinian activist at his home," *Los Angeles Times,* April 10, 2024, https://www.latimes.com/california /story/2024-04-10/uc-berkeley-law-school-dean-clashes-with-pro-palestinian -activists.

32. We could imagine some complications with viewpoint-based or content-based uses of trespass law, but life is hard enough already, so let's not.

33. This scenario is based on highly publicized activities at Columbia University in April, 2024. Still, it is intended to be hypothetical, and it is not meant as a report on what happened at that time.

34. United States v. O'Brien, 391 U.S. 367 (1968).

35. *O'Brien,* 391 U.S. at 377.

36. See *Rosenberger,* 515 U.S. at 829.

37. Mahanoy Area Sch. Dist. v. B.L. *ex rel.* Levy, 141 S. Ct. 2038, 2045 (2021) (noting that the "special characteristics" of schools call for "special leeway when schools regulate speech that occurs under its supervision"). See also Tinker v. Des Moines Indep. Cmty. Sch. Dist., 393 U.S. 503, 513 (1969) (noting that schools have a special interest in regulating speech that "materially disrupts classwork or involves substantial disorder or invasion of the rights of others"); *Grayned,* 408 U.S. at 119 (school's prohibition of speech that "disrupts or is about to disrupt normal school activities" was lawful under First Amendment, because school had compelling interest in "having an undisrupted school session conducive to the students' learning").

38. Cohen v. California, 403 U.S. 15, 22–23 (1971) (states may not punish "public utterance[s] of . . . unseemly expletive[s] in order to maintain what they regard as a suitable level of discourse within the body politic").

39. *Cohen*, 403 U.S. at 22–23; see also Mahanoy Area Sch. Dist. v. B.L. *ex rel.* Levy, 141 S. Ct. 2038, 2049 n.2 (Alito, J., concurring) (noting differences between college students and primary and secondary students).

40. Bethel Sch. Dist. No. 403 v. Fraser, 478 U.S. 675 (1986).

41. *Bethel*, 478 U.S. at 681. The Court continued: "[T]he First Amendment gives a high school student the classroom right to wear Tinker's armband, but not Cohen's jacket." *Bethel*, 478 U.S. at 682 (quoting Thomas v. Board of Education, Granville Central School Dist., 607 F.2d 1043, 1057 (2d Cir. 1979) (Newman, J., concurring in the judgment)).

42. *Bethel*, 478 U.S. at 683.

43. Papish v. Bd. of Curators of Univ. of Mo., 410 U.S. 667 (1973).

44. *Papish*, 410 U.S. at 672.

45. *Rosenberger*, 515 U.S. at 829 ("The government must abstain from regulating speech when the specific motivating ideology or the opinion or perspective of the speaker is the rationale for the restriction.").

46. *Rosenberger*, 515 U.S. at 831.

47. *Rosenberger*, 515 U.S. at 836.

48. See Rust v. Sullivan, 500 U.S. 173 (1991), on the topic of government funding in general.

49. It is one thing to say that to repress speech, officials must meet the *Brandenburg* test; that is established law. (I am continuing to bracket the possibility that in the educational setting, the *Brandenburg* test should be somewhat softened—as when, for example, there is a 45 percent chance of imminent lawless action, rather than a 51 percent chance of imminent lawless action.) But it is another thing to say that funding may not be denied to an organization specifically created to promote illegality; that is not established law. Still, we have to be careful here; what about the Organization to Promote Civil Disobedience? Or the Organization to Promote Civil Disobedience in Honor of Martin Luther King, Jr.?

3. Professors

1. McLaughlin v. Fla. Int'l Univ. Bd. of Trs., 533 F. Supp. 3d 1149, 1177 (S.D. Fla. 2021), *aff'd*, No. 21-11453, 2022 WL 1203080 (11th Cir. Apr. 22, 2022) (rejecting First Amendment claim alleging that law professor's left-wing views unconstitutionally chilled speech of conservative student, causing her "subjective discomfort").

2. United States v. Schwimmer, 279 U.S. 644, 655 (1929) (Holmes, J., dissenting).

3. Pickering v. Bd. of Educ., 391 U.S. 563 (1968); See Chapter 1 for discussion of the case facts.

4. Heim v. Daniel, 81 F.4th 212, 233 (2d Cir. 2023) ("[I]n nearly all contexts, government officials are barred from discriminating among speakers based on their own judgments of the quality or content of the speech").

5. See *Heim*, 81 F.4th at 234 (concluding that university officials did not violate First Amendment when denying adjunct professor tenure on the basis of his methodological choices). As the court explained, "decision-makers within a university must be permitted to consider the content of an aspiring faculty member's academic speech, and to make judgments informed by their own scholarly views, when making academic appointments." *Heim*, 81 F.4th at 234. See also Lopez v. Bd. of Trustees of Univ. of Illinois at Chicago, 344 F. Supp. 2d 611, 623 (N.D. Ill. 2004) (rejecting First Amendment retaliation claim arising from university's denial of tenure due to concerns about "the quality of [the professor's] scholarship").

6. Piggee v. Carl Sandburg Coll., 464 F.3d 667, 672 (7th Cir. 2006) (holding that First Amendment did not protect cosmetology teacher's religious proselytization in class, and explaining that the "college reasonably took the position that nongermane discussions of religion and other matters had no place in the classroom, because they could impede the school's educational mission").

7. *Pickering*, 391 U.S. 563 (1968); Connick v. Myers, 461 U.S. 138 (1983). Connick v. Myers, 461 U.S. 138 (1983). See Chapter 1 for discussion of how

Pickering and *Connick* together distinguish between government employee rights by asking if government employers are acting as employers or as government entities.

8. In *Pickering,* one key factor was that the teacher's published comments were not related to internal school operations. See *Pickering,* 391 U.S. at 572 ("We are . . . not presented with a situation in which a teacher has carelessly made false statements about matters . . . closely related to the day-to-day operations of the schools").

9. Soglin v. Kauffman, 418 F.2d 163 (7th Cir. 1969) (requiring rules to be specific enough to give notice of what is allowable behavior).

10. Martin v. Parrish, 805 F.2d 583 (5th Cir. 1986) (holding, on application of *Connick,* that college professor had no First Amendment right to "cuss[ ] out" students in the classroom).

11. *Martin,* 805 F.2d at 583.

12. Hardy v. Jefferson Cmty. Coll., 260 F.3d 671, 679 (6th Cir. 2001) (holding that college professor's use of the "n-word" in a lecture relating to interpersonal communication was constitutionally protected because it was "germane to the subject matter of his lecture on the power and effect of language").

13. Berger v. Battaglia, 779 F.2d 992, 999 (4th Cir. 1985) (holding that police officer's off-duty public performances in blackface were protected by the First Amendment such that employer could not retaliate against him). The *Battaglia* court further noted that "[a]n appropriate . . . response, perhaps the only one, wholly consistent with the [F]irst [A]mendment, would have been . . . to say to those offended by [the police officer's] speech that their right to protest that speech by all peaceable means would be . . . stringently safeguarded." *Battaglia* 779 F.2d at 1001.

14. See the discussion in R.A.V. v. City of St. Paul, 505 U.S. 377 (1992): "Thus, for example, sexually derogatory 'fighting words,' among other words, may produce a violation of Title VII's general prohibition against sexual discrimination in employment practices. Where the government does not target conduct on the basis of its expressive content, acts are not shielded from regulation merely because they express a discriminatory idea or philosophy."

The conclusion in text follows from Robinson v. Jacksonville Shipyards, Inc., 760 F. Supp. 1486 (M.D. Fla. 1991); Davis v. Monsanto Chem. Co., 858 F.2d 345, 350 (6th Cir.1988), *cert. denied,* 490 U.S. 1110 (1989); Jew v. University of Iowa, 749 F. Supp. 946, 961 (S.D. Iowa 1990).

15. 303 Creative LLC v. Elenis, 600 U.S. 570, 597 (2023) (arguing that the line between expressive conduct and speech is elusive and perhaps nonexistent). I am bracketing some complicated issues here, involving "doing things with words" and the idea of speech acts. If Oedipus says the words, "I do," during a wedding ceremony involving his mother and himself, he is committing an illegal act.

16. Compare with Davis *ex rel.* LaShonda D. v. Monroe Cnty. Bd. of Educ., 526 U.S. 629, 667 (1999) (Kennedy, J., dissenting) ("A university's power to discipline its students for speech that may constitute sexual harassment is also circumscribed by the First Amendment").

17. Bd. of Educ., Island Trees Union Free Sch. Dist. No. 26 v. Pico, 457 U.S. 853 (1982).

18. *Pico,* 457 U.S. at 870.

19. *Pico,* 457 U.S. at 871.

20. *Pico,* 457 U.S. at 871.

21. *Pico,* 457 U.S. at 871.

22. *Pico,* 457 U.S. at 884.

23. *Pico,* 457 U.S. 853.

24. *Pico,* 457 U.S. at 870; see also Keyishian v. Bd. of Regents of Univ. of State of N.Y., 385 U.S. 589, 603, 87 S. Ct. 675, 683, 17 L. Ed. 2d 629 (1967) ("[T]he First Amendment . . . does not tolerate laws that cast a pall of orthodoxy over the classroom.").

25. *Pico,* 457 U.S. 853.

26. See, e.g., Lawrence B. Solum, "The Public Meaning Thesis: An Originalist Theory of Constitutional Meaning," *Boston University Law Review* 101, no. 6 (Dec. 2021): 1953–2048.

27. See, e.g., Ronald Dworkin, *Freedom's Law: The Moral Reading of the American Constitution* (Cambridge, MA: Harvard University Press, 1997).

28. See Taylor Swift, "Mean," track 6 on *Speak Now (Taylor's Version)*, Republic Records, 2023.

29. See, e.g., Dube v. State Univ. of N.Y., 900 F.2d 587 (2d Cir. 1990) (finding that if a university retaliated against a professor because of public reaction to the content of his class, the professor's First Amendment rights were violated).

30. See, e.g., Pernell v. Fla. Bd. of Governors of the State Univ. Sys., 641 F. Supp. 3d 1218, 1242, 1277 (N.D. Fla. 2022) (arguing that a "professor cannot decide to teach something entirely different or do an end-run around the prescribed curriculum by paying lip service to the subject they are supposed to teach and then spend the rest of class time instructing on something else," and that "'academic freedom' does not justify a professor hijacking their class discussion to focus on matters outside the established curriculum"); Buchanan v. Alexander, 919 F.3d 847, 854 (5th Cir. 2019) (holding that in-class speech that is "clearly not related to" the subject of the class is not protected); Edwards v. Calif. Univ., 156 F.3d 488, 491 (3d Cir. 1998) ("we conclude that a public university professor does not have a First Amendment right to decide what will be taught in the classroom"); *Piggee,* 464 F.3d at 671("No college or university is required to allow a chemistry professor to devote extensive classroom time to the teaching of James Joyce's demanding novel *Ulysses,* nor must it permit a professor of mathematics to fill her class hours with instruction on the law of torts.").

31. See, e.g., *Heim,* 81 F.4th at 232–234 (describing the many factors that universities may consider in making hiring decisions); Curtis v. Univ. of Houston, 940 F. Supp. 1070, 1075 (S.D. Tex. 1996) (describing the tenure decision as the "inherently subjective" consideration of "myriad . . . factors about which the court can only speculate").

32. See Epperson v. Arkansas, 393 U.S. 97, 116 (1968) (Stewart, J., concurring in the result) ("The States are most assuredly free 'to choose their own curriculums for their own schools.' A state is entirely free, for example, to decide that the only foreign language to be taught in its public school system shall be Spanish."); see also *Epperson,* 393 U.S. at 111 (Black, J., concurring) ("It

would be difficult to make a First Amendment case out of a state law eliminating the subject of higher mathematics, or astronomy, or biology from its curriculum.").

33. See *Heim*, 81 F.4th at 214, 234 ("we disagree with the legal theory . . . that, under the First Amendment, a public university's hiring decisions cannot be informed by methodological preference . . . decision-makers within a university must be permitted to consider the content of an aspiring faculty member's academic speech, and to make judgments informed by their own scholarly views, when making academic appointments").

34. *Pico*, 457 U.S. 853.

35. This is based on an actual case. See Campbell Robertson and Anna Betts, "Indiana Law Requires Professors to Promote 'Intellectual Diversity' or Face Penalties," *New York Times*, March 23, 2024, https://www.nytimes.com /2024/03/23/us/indiana-professors-tenure-diversity.html.

36. See Reno v. Am. C.L. Union, 521 U.S. 844 (1997) (prohibiting restrictions of speech that amount to a heckler's veto).

37. !

4. Public and Private

1. Mary Hui, "Georgetown Students Have Filed a Discrimination Complaint Against a Campus Group Promoting Heterosexual Marriage," *Washington Post*, Oct. 25, 2017, https://www.washingtonpost.com/news/acts-of-faith /wp/2017/10/25/georgetown-students-file-a-discrimination-complaint -against-a-campus-group-that-promotes-heterosexual-marriage/.

2. Lindsay Cates, "College Road Trip to Boston: Boston College," *U.S. News & World Report*, Sept. 28, 2020, https://www.usnews.com/education /best-colleges/articles/college-road-trip-to-boston-boston-college.

3. W. Va. State Bd. of Educ. v. Barnette, 319 U.S. 624, 641 (1943).

4. For example, Brigham Young University restricts student demonstrations that "contradict or oppose, rather than analyze or discuss, fundamental Church doctrine or policy" or "deliberately attack or deride the Church or

its general leaders." See "Demonstration Policy," Brigham Young University, approved Mar. 25, 2024, https://policy.byu.edu/view/demonstration-policy. By contrast, Notre Dame allows students and faculty to "express their views on any matter" even if "some of the views expressed may not accord with principles of Catholic teaching." See "Freedom of Expression at Notre Dame," Rev. John I. Jenkins, C.S.C, Notre Dame, Feb. 20, 2023, https://president.nd.edu/homilies-writings-addresses/freedom-of-expression-at-notre-dame/.

5. See Parker v. Levy, 417 U.S. 733, 758 (1974) ("While the members of the military are not excluded from the protection granted by the First Amendment, the different character of the military community and of the military mission requires a different application of those protections. The fundamental necessity for obedience, and the consequent necessity for imposition of discipline, may render permissible within the military that which would be constitutionally impermissible outside it.").

6. Office of the Commandant, U.S. Military Academy, "USCC Policy Memorandum 15: Professional Online Conduct," (n.d.): 2.

7. "USCC Policy Memorandum," 3–4.

8. U.S. Naval Academy, *The Blue and Gold Book* (n.d.).

9. Office of the Commandant of Midshipmen, U.S. Naval Academy, "Commandant of Midshipmen Instruction 5400.6V," (2019): 3-1.

10. "Commandant of Midshipmen," 4-1.

11. "Commandant of Midshipmen," 4-2.

12. "Commandant of Midshipmen," 4-3.

13. Grayned v. City of Rockford, 408 U.S. 104 (1972).

14. See, e.g., Soglin v. Kauffman, 418 F.2d 163 (7th Cir. 1969).

5. Taking Sides

1. Kalven Committee, *Report on the University's Role in Political and Social Action* (Chicago: University of Chicago, 1967), https://provost.uchicago.edu/reports/report-universitys-role-political-and-social-action.

2. See "Recommendation that the Dep't of Just. Not Defend the Constitutionality of Certain Provisions of the Bankr. Amends. and Fed. Judgeship Act of 1984," 8 Op. O.L.C. 183, 195 (1984) (no duty to defend statutes that "usurp executive authority and therefore weaken the President's constitutional role").

6. Let Freedom Ring

1. Of course there are antecedents. Cass R. Sunstein, "Free Speech Now," *University of Chicago Law Review* 59, no. 1 (1992): 255–316.

2. See, e.g., Geoffrey R. Stone, "Content-Neutral Restrictions," *University of Chicago Law Review* 54, no. 1 (1987): 58 ("the Court generally tests content-neutral restrictions with an implicit balancing approach: the greater the interference with the marketplace of ideas, the greater the burden on government to justify the restriction").

Acknowledgments

I am grateful to many people for their help. Thanks first and foremost to Geoffrey Stone, a beloved friend and a guide on all things, including the First Amendment (on free speech, he is the best of the best). It is an honor to walk in his footsteps. I thank him for valuable discussions and comments. For the same, many thanks to Benjamin Eidelson, Elizabeth Emens, Richard Fallon, Noah Feldman, Marty Lederman, Martha Minow, Steven Pinker, Robert Post, and Eugene Volokh. Special thanks to Andy Gu, Ethan Judd, Thomas Nielsen, and Victoria Yu for valuable comments and superb research assistance. Applause in particular to Yu for helping to shepherd the book to completion.

Sarah Chalfant, my amazing agent, was essential to the whole project. At Harvard University Press, George Andreou saw, early on, that there might be a book here, and Grigory Tovbis offered a host of terrific suggestions, which made the book broader and better (and less little). Katrina Vassallo was a tremendous copyeditor. Heartfelt thanks to each and all.

Index